Make Every
Minute Count

Make Every Minute Count

More than 700 Tips
and Strategies That Will
Revolutionize How You
Manage Your Time

HARLAN LANE, PH.D., AND CHRISTIAN WAYSER

MARLOWE & COMPANY
NEW YORK

Published by
Marlowe & Company
A Division of Avalon Publishing Group Incorporated
841 Broadway
New York, NY 10003

MAKE EVERY MINUTE COUNT: *More than 700 Tips and Strategies That Will Revolutionize How You Manage Your Time*

LIBRARY OF CONGRESS CATALOGING-IN-PUBLICATION DATA
Lane, Harlan L.
    Make every minute count : more than 700 tips and strategies to
    revolutionize how you manage your time / Harlan Lane and
    Christian Wayser.
        p. cm.
    ISBN 1-56924-613-0
    1. Time management.   2. Strategic planning.   I. Wayser,
    Christian.   II. Title.

HD69.T54 L36 2000
650.1—dc21
                                                          00-056847

9 8 7 6 5 4 3 2 1

Designed by Pauline Neuwirth, Neuwirth & Associates, Inc.

Printed in the United States of America
Distributed by Publishers Group West

Contents

1. General Strategies for Saving Time   5

Do you want to reduce the time you spend waiting, take control of your schedule, and get the decisions you want from others more quickly? In this chapter, you'll find advice on these and dozens of other general strategies in 136 helpful tips. We'll guide you in reviewing your personal and professional goals, so you can see whether you are spending time as you want to. We'll give you painless methods for getting organized and staying that way with tips on making lists, sequencing tasks, doing two things at once, and more. Here, too, is advice on practicing good time management with other people such as delegating, saying "no," and dealing with procrastination.

2. Business   52

Appointments and meetings can help you achieve your goals—or they can squander your precious time. Learn here how to schedule them, how to keep them short and productive, and how to handle interruptions. The more than 50 tips here offer advice on meals and business, organizing your office, filing, and time-wise ways of dealing with employees, peers and supervisors. (Also see Communications, Computers, and Travel.)

Includes Checklist for Office supplies (Tip #188).

3. Communications 70

Cellular phones, faxes, pagers, e-mail—there are so many new ways to communicate today. Knowing when and how to use them—along with the classic telephone and the mail—makes the difference between saving time and losing time. More than 50 tips will guide you in this chapter.

4. Computers and the Internet 89

For everyone who has a checkbook or appointments to keep, the most valuable tool for good time management today is the computer, yet many people don't take advantage of this tool because they are not sure what equipment and programs to buy. This chapter with more than 50 tips explains the many things a computer can do to help you save time, and it offers expert advice on what to choose, how to buy it, how to get technical help, and how to arrange your computer workspace for safety and efficiency. Learn here about the new palmtops, laptops, and desktops. Lots of tips on the Internet, from how to get connected to time-saving Internet addresses; books and banking to entertainment, health and much more.

5. Food 113

Three meals a day often take up more time than we have, especially when shopping for food, preparing it, and cleaning up are included. Shopping lists are helpful—ours is the best one we've seen yet. We also have tips to offer on choosing kitchen equipment, shopping and preparing food. Here, too, are time-saving menus and recipes for quick and easy meals. And a special treat: fast French recipes from French culinary authority Jean-Pierre Coffe. 86 tips to make meals tasty and time-wise.

Includes Checklist for Shopping (Tip #386).

6. Health and Recreation 140

Americans have become more conscious of the importance of staying fit and living a healthy lifestyle, but it is difficult to find the time for all that's involved. This chapter tells you how to get the maximum benefit in the least time from your fitness regime, what it should include, and what to buy. There are time-wise tips on reducing stress, taking vacations, and fitting sleep into a hectic life. We also offer tips on how to save time with doctor's appointments, prescriptions, and emergencies. Look over our tips on time-conscious ways to keep up with old friends, meet other people, find a romantic partner, socialize while dining, and to fit recreation into your life, including spectator sports, parties, and movies — 73 tips in all.

Includes Checklist for Parties (Tip #420).

7. Home 167

This chapter has 167 tips on how to save time at home. Time pressure on the family is greater than ever before as more women enter the workforce. Parents who are in search of time-saving tips to manage children's meals, clothing, laundry, transportation and recreation will find dozens here along with tips on infant care, delegating chores, planning family events, caring for pets, and governing ungovernable children. We have covered every room in the house, giving time-wise tips for cleaning, storage, and shopping for appliances, furnishings and clothing. Save time when doing the laundry, dressing and grooming. Here are tips, too, on home entertainment, home maintenance, repairs, security, insurance and moving. Check out our list of essential tools for the home. Every home is also a kind of business, and we have tips on organizing your home office, on filing and supplies, on bill paying, and banking. There's even a list of the most common disasters in life, with tips on how to avoid them and save time when they do occur.

Includes Checklists for Appliances and Utensils (Tip #536), Tools (Tip #575), Home Filing (Tip #591), and Supplies (Tip #607).

8. Travel 215

Transportation is a "black hole" that sucks up time and money, whether commuting in a car or flying to another city. We can help with more than 80 tips. Here you will find advice on how to select and buy a car, maintain it, and deal with all the time hassles, such as licenses, traffic and parking. See our checklist of important items to keep in your car. Smart flight planning can save a lot of time, too. We offer checklists for selecting flights and for packing, and advice on choosing airports, speeding through airport check-in and making connections. Hotels are full of unpleasant surprises but not if you use our checklist and advice on hotel booking. Prefer trains, buses and taxis? There are tips here to help you save time with those modes of transportation too.

Includes Checklists for What to Have in Your Car (Tip #665), Packing (Tip #675), Flights (Tip #687), and Business Trips (Tip #700).

Introduction

More than ever, people are feeling short of time. Half the people responding to a 1995 Gallup poll said they do not have enough time to do what they want to do and the same fraction told *U.S. News and World Report* they would pick more time over more money if given the choice. (It would be nice to have the choice.)

If you belong to the fifty percent who are feeling **short of time** and are ready to take action, **we can help**. After all, you manage your money, your health and your grooming, why not manage your time? We can't tell you how to save time literally—there's no way to store it away—but we can help you change how you spend your time, so that more of it goes to the activities that are important to you. What would you do with the gift of a few more hours each day for you to use as you wish? Spend the time with your family? Earn more money? Train to compete in triathlons? Learn a new language? Read a book? (Or even write one.) Meditate? Volunteer for a worthy cause? The possibilities are endless.

Once you gain control of your time, you will find that there is **less stress** in your life. Stress arises when you are trying to get something perfectly reasonable done and some idiot (or situation created by idiots) is stopping you. Say, you're in a restaurant trying to catch your waiter's eye so you can get to a show on time, but your waiter persistently looks the other way, as if you were engaged in some unseemly act. Or you're trying to catch a flight, but the line snaking its way to the ticket counter resembles the exodus from Egypt. Or, you're trying to correct an error in your electricity bill but the company's telephone answering system has more baffling menu choices than a nightmare set in a Chinese restaurant. We will show you how to avoid getting caught in such squeezes, and how to wiggle out if you do get caught.

Profit-hungry businesses and economy-minded government are wasting more of our time than ever before. No wonder you feel short of time! But **you're not to blame—they are**. The airline that leaves you waiting on hold hires fewer customer agents and makes an extra buck at your expense. The doctor who keeps you sitting in the waiting room sees more patients in a day and makes an extra buck at your expense. So does the repair service that doesn't keep its appointments, the supermarket with too few cashiers, the store with untrained salespeople—there's a long list. As more and more companies and agencies leverage off your time, your need to take charge of your time is greater than ever.

We give you ways to fight back, help not only managing your time but managing the behavior of others who spend your time for their purposes. We'll help you deal with anonymous systems that waste your time with their toadies: Ms. Fill-These-In, who finds pure joy in putting obstacles in your path; Mr. Meany who, bullied by his wife at night, takes revenge on you the next morning; Ms. Overwhelmed, whose eyes plead for sympathy; Mr. I'm-Sorry, who clearly isn't—and the rest of their ilk.

In addition to showing you how you can influence those who are consuming your time, this book also offers a wide-ranging **treasury of time-saving tips** and strategies to apply in many areas of your life. It's the only time-saving book you'll ever need. We have included over 700 tips, the best from Europe and America, many drawn from our own personal experience. There are chapters on health, home, food, communication, travel, the office— eight chapters and over seventy topics. Tailor the book to your own situation. First, turn to the chapters that particularly concern you. Within each chapter, the tips are arranged by topic. The clock ⏰ signals a time-saving tip (for example, how to fit fitness into your day). The magnifier 🔍 indicates an in-depth look at a major time-saving theme (such as how to delegate household chores). The helm ☸ calls attention to our advice on how to influence others (and yourself) to save time. Many tips come with benefits and burdens, pros 👍 and cons 👎 worth noting. And sometimes we warn you when we think that following a tip might cost you too much in life's pleasures ⚖. Scan the topics, try carrying out the tips that suit you, while using others and the many lists just as reminders, and ignore those tips that don't apply or appeal to you. You will find it is easy and painless to gain control of your time.

Many of the tips in this book you knew all along, or could have figured out for yourself if you had the inclination and time. We offer practical solutions that are within your reach, so it is natural that they often seem a matter of common sense. What we have done for you is to organize your knowledge of time-saving strategies and tactics, to expand it, and to provide you with numerous reminders and a guide for reflecting on how you spend your time. If most of our suggestions make sense to you and you wonder why you didn't put them into practice before, so much the better.

We know that our lives are more productive and pleasant thanks to these time-saving tips and strategies. We believe yours will be, too. Please be assured: we do not profit in any way from the products and services we recommend. We'd love to hear from you. Use the response form at the end of the book to give us feedback and to share new tips or strategies. (Of course, we'll acknowledge those we use.) Time-wise citizens working together could make life in our society a lot more pleasant and productive.

A FINAL NOTE: All the information, including brand names, model numbers and costs, website addresses and telephone numbers, were accurate to the best of our knowledge at the time of printing. To be most useful, the information is detailed. Please be aware that such details change.

General Strategies for Saving Time

BACKUP

1. Backup plan Life is full of mishaps; they'll waste less of ⏱ your time if you have a backup plan.

- When arranging to meet someone at the airport, have a backup plan in case you miss one another.
- Bring some work or leisure reading to appointments, in case you arrive early or your contact is late.
- Backup your computer files nightly (see Computers-Software-Backup) and keep a master monthly backup in another location.
- When seeking someone's consent (for example, to a promotion) have a backup plan in case your request is denied.

"ALL CHANCE, DIRECTION WHICH THOU CANST NOT SEE"
(ALEXANDER POPE)

2. Buy double Your car has a spare tire so you won't be strand- ⏱ ed. For the same reason, shouldn't you have spare eyeglasses, computers (a laptop perhaps), even a car in reserve? We're not urging you to buy another Maserati, just to take backup into account when considering a second car for spouse, children or others.

3. Important numbers It is prudent to write down all important numbers in a secure place:

- credit cards
- "PIN" numbers
- combination locks
- unlisted telephone numbers
- product ID numbers for software
- username and passwords for websites, email accounts and computers in a network.

CANDOR

4. Asking questions If you don't understand an explanation and it is not important, you may save time by pretending you understand when you do not. However, if you need the explanation, you will save time by asking questions. Since you can't think of every question, it's wise to end up with "Thanks. Is there anything else I need to know about this?"

"ASK, AND YE SHALL RECEIVE, THAT YOUR JOY MAY BE FULL."
(THE GOSPEL ACCORDING TO SAINT JOHN)

5. Complaints When a company representative is wasting your time, it is a good policy to tell him or her so.

"EVEN GOD LENDS A HAND TO HONEST BOLDNESS."
(MENANDER C. 342–292 B.C.)

It is an even better policy to put your complaint in writing. After all, how can companies reform their practices if they do not receive feedback of this sort?

EXAMPLE: A restaurant fails to honor your reservation. Tell the manager why you are disappointed and not inclined to return.

TIME-SAVING TIP   INFLUENCE   FOCUS

Companies appreciate feedback; they know that most wronged customers will stick with the company if there is reform.

 This is an important mode of social action to improve everyone's quality of life. You will feel better having done something constructive; and you may learn something useful (e.g., times to avoid).

 It takes a moment to complain, especially in writing, and it can be awkward in person.

6. Time consciousness
If you are a businessman, manager, or service provider, an important way to establish good relations with your customers is to acknowledge the value of their time and to behave accordingly.

When there is an occasional and unavoidable delay, be candid, explain why it arose, and what will be done to avoid a recurrence. This tells the clients that you respect them: you would no more intrude on their time than on their space.

 Greater client loyalty; a broader client base; more cordial client relations.

 Respect for client time may entail higher operating costs.

7. Time constraints

"HURRY UP PLEASE IT'S TIME."
(T. S. ELIOT)

One of the most important ways to save time is to be candid about it. Tell the appointments secretary, the visitor, the friend that it is important to you to begin and end on time because of your other commitments.

Since so many people behave as if time were of no importance—waiting over an hour to be seated in a restaurant, standing patiently on long lines at the airport and so on—you cannot take it for granted that others will be respectful of your time, unless you tell them about your needs.

CHOICES

⏰ **8. Environment** The environment that you choose or create at home or at your place of business affects productivity and time management.

- If you can, set aside a space exclusively for your work.
- Provide the necessary furniture and devices (computer, file cabinets, etc.).
- Position your desk so the outside lighting is suitable for work and provide adequate indoor lighting.
- Warm colors, such as red and orange are exciting, yellows are cheerful, while greens and blues are restful.

⏰ **9. Giving up** There are limits to what you can do. If you haven't found the time in many months to pursue some goal, perhaps it isn't as important as you thought and you should give it up.

👍 Relief that you gave up.

👎 Disappointment that you gave up.

⏰ **10. Make it simple** Standard is faster to order and more likely to be correct: standard invitations, checks, deli platters, computer configurations, etc.

⏰ **11. Memberships** Many small concessions make a large burden: Do not agree lightly to run errands, serve nominally on boards, join a club, make calls for someone else, read their magnum opus, walk their dog, move their furniture, host their cousin.

👍 More time to spend on your priorities.

👎 It is hard to refuse individual modest requests.

⏰ TIME-SAVING TIP   INFLUENCE   FOCUS

12. Priorities

Busy people who value their time have little to spare for empty gestures. Pick spheres of action where you can have a demonstrable effect and restrict your activities primarily to those.

> "THE TIME OF LIFE IS SHORT; TO SPEND THAT SHORTNESS BASELY WERE TOO LONG."
>
> (SHAKESPEARE)

13. Questions to ask

Journalists are taught to ask Who What Where When and How. These are good questions for querying your activities:

WHO is the right person to do this task?
WHAT is the task exactly?
WHERE will the activity best be carried out?
WHEN is the best time to schedule it?
HOW could this be accomplished faster, smarter?
And we add:
WHY are you bothering? How is it necessary?

14. Shopping

Limiting your choices to a small number of businesses and service providers saves time.

Places you patronize repeatedly come to know you and your needs; your data are probably in their computer, expediting your order. If you seek redress for an error or some special service, your standing as their regular customer will help.

15. Time of day

What is your best time of day for serious work? Some people say early morning; others are night owls. If you can, play to your strength and organize your work day accordingly.

① 16. Your civic duty

"TIME IS THE MOST VALUABLE THING A MAN CAN SPEND."
(THEOPHRASTUS)

What would our society be like if people wouldn't stand on line or sit in waiting areas (except in emergencies); if we all hung up when placed on hold or when confronted with lengthy telephone menus; if we made our communal anger over traffic snarls known to municipal government; if we all left when a restaurant didn't honor reservations? The answer is: If we refused to let our time be wasted, companies and governments would waste less of our time. They would adopt more efficient practices, hire more people, place more value on time savings in planning. Some things might cost a little more, or their shareholders might earn a few a dollars less, but wouldn't life be grand without lines, telephone menus, holds and snarls?

Clearly, changing the world for the better in this way requires large numbers of people refusing to have their time wasted. So it is your civic duty to refuse to let your time be wasted. When you allow your time to be exploited for someone else's profit, you not only waste your time, you perpetuate bad practices that waste everybody's time.

DELEGATING

① 17. Benefits
Delegate all that you can. Not only will you save time, you may find that the person you entrusted with the task has a fresh vision, or skills that complement your own.

☌ 18. Confidence levels
A manager is a person responsible for getting a job done with the help of others. If you are a mother, a team captain, or a businessman or businesswoman, you are probably a manager.

As a manager, you can save time by delegating but you incur the risk that the task will not be carried out as you would have done it. The trick is to choose the right level of confidence in

TIME-SAVING TIP   INFLUENCE

FOCUS

your assistant, knowing the task, that person's qualifications, and the penalty you will pay if he or she doesn't get it right.

The following instructions when delegating show the six levels of confidence and of time savings, from least to most:

1. Assemble the facts and give them to me. I will make the decision and take action.
2. Assemble and study the facts. Recommend an action for my approval.
3. Assemble and study the facts and take action but check with me first.
4. Assemble and study the facts and take action; notify me so I can intervene if I want to.
5. Assemble and study the facts and take action. Report to me afterwards on what you did.
6. Assemble and study the facts and take action. No need to report.

19. Hiring Hire other people to do some things for you. ⏲

- It will spare you chores you do not like and give you time you can reallocate to your priorities.
- You may come out money ahead, since the time you freed up is available for activities that make you money or save you money.

👍 Time and perhaps money, and relief from tasks not to your taste.

👎 Expense, finding the right person.

20. Logging With the goal of delegating some of your activities in mind, note on your calendar during one week how you spent each hour. ⏲

Group the notes into categories (commuting, cleaning, writing, shopping . . .) and total the hours.

- Are there activities you can delegate to others?
- Are they in your family or your workgroup, or do you need to hire a company or a person?

BENEFITS

BURDENS

BALANCE

- If you engage in many short activities, use shorter intervals than an hour, to see the total time that those scattered activities take from your schedule.

 21. Money matters Delegate your signature for invoices and routine checks and documents.

 22. Self-assessment Why do we fail so often to delegate duties to others—even duties they would gladly fulfill? Don't let these barriers to delegating waste your time:

FOCUS ON BARRIERS TO DELEGATING

BARRIER #1. I don't trust them to do it correctly.
- Choose the right person for the task, give them the information and authority they require to accomplish it, and set up a system for monitoring progress.

BARRIER #2. I'd like full credit for accomplishing this task.
- Failing to delegate some tasks can interfere with your accomplishing and getting credit for others.
- Good teamwork can reflect better on a manager than a superb solo performance.
- When you give up some of the credit, you give up some of the risk.

BARRIER #3. Subordinates keep referring minor and major issues back to me.
- With carefully worded guidelines and illustrative examples, clarify for them the range of decisions you want them to make.

DEVICES

 23. Domestic brands Buy domestic brands, other things being equal. It is generally easier to get repair parts and service and technical advice for devices made domestically.

TIME-SAVING TIP

INFLUENCE

FOCUS

24. Friends Buy brands your friends know and recommend.
They can testify to their merits and drawbacks and can advise you
on their use.

25. Gadgets Thank heavens for gadgets—they make life so
much more pleasant and effective and save time, too. We are
thinking of those devices people use every day, such as vacuum
cleaners, electric toothbrushes, computers, food processors, automatic coffee makers.

Buy gadgets! But don't buy ones that you will use rarely—battery operated swizzle sticks, cherry pit removers, electrical tie
racks. They take up space, add to the clutter and cost money.

26. Learning to use People who think life is plug-and-
play are often frustrated. Read the manual first before operating
your new answering machine, computer, car or other device. You
will reduce your risk of damaging the device, you will learn
shortcuts and options you might otherwise overlook, and it is
often faster in the long run.

27. Manuals When acquiring a new device, be it a video
recorder, a power tool, or software, for example, get as much tute-
lage from salespeople and tech support as you can. Save related
documents and manuals carefully—you will need them. We keep
a three-ring binder next to each computer and collect in it copies
of all invoices for software and hardware, notes from conversations with tech support, rescue diskettes in case of a hard drive
failure, and a printout of system properties.

28. Mnemonics Devices and the Internet frequently
require code numbers or passwords. Ideally, we could use the
same number or password for all vendors but no such luck: each
vendor imposes different restrictions on the length and content of
the numbers.

- You can keep a list of those numbers handy but it is faster to
  learn them with a mnemonic. For example, suppose your
  PIN number is 1945—that's the year WWII ended in

Europe. It's also 19 and 45, which may be the ages of your niece and sister, or the street addresses of one or two acquaintances, etc. Also, there is one 9, and the remaining two numbers sum to 9.

29. Single manufacturer
Buy ensembles from a single manufacturer; the components are more likely to work well together. And when something goes wrong, the manufacturer of component A cannot fob you off on another manufacturer by blaming the problem on their component B.

DO IT NOW

30. 4-D method
The 4-D approach to work saves time:

> Dump some.
> Delay some.
> Delegate some.
> Do the rest now.

31. Doubling Up
Some of the best ideas arise when you are horizontal. Keep a pad and pencil next to your bed. If issues are troubling you, write those down, too, and they will go on hold more readily.

32. Filing
- Don't file recipes, correspondence, documents immediately, it is more efficient to file when there is a quantity of documents in your to-file box.
- Filing is a good activity to use for doubling up or filling fragmented time. For example, if you are put on hold, press the speakerphone button and do a little filing.
- Don't let things pile up too much, though; you run the risk of having to search for them both in the file and in the to-file box.

TIME-SAVING TIP

INFLUENCE

FOCUS

33. Listen first Under the pressure of do-it-now, we some-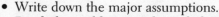
times start solving the problem before understanding it fully. If
the problem's complex:

- Write down the major assumptions.
- Break the problem into logical elements.
- Define your broad strategy.
- Set our your detailed plan.
- Solicit advice as appropriate.
- Estimate costs and potential gains.
- Do it.

34. Perfectionism Some perfectionists procrastinate.
Example: They can't find the perfect gift, so they end up with
none at all.

Others waste time by continuing beyond completion. With
more time and effort, almost everything can be improved, so
completing projects means knowing when to let go.

"LET ME DO IT NOW; LET ME NOT DEFER OR NEGLECT IT, FOR
I SHALL NOT PASS THIS WAY AGAIN."

(PROVERB)

35. Procrastination "Procrastination is the thief of
time," says the poet and anyone who has shopped the day before
Christmas knows he is right.

Two steps will help when dealing with people who procrastinate (including yourself):

- Discover what rewards and punishments are fueling the procrastination;
- Change them if you can.

People procrastinate performing a task because:

- What they are doing instead is more rewarding. Reduce the
  rewards.
- The task is unpleasant. Make it more pleasant, perhaps reas-
  signing parts of it.
- They fear failure when carrying it out. Help them approach
  it gradually and safely.

- They fear what will follow completing the task. Help them express and explore that fear.
- They like being cajoled: it shows you care. Stop cajoling them.

36. Procrastination How do you eat an elephant? One bite at a time. Break the daunting task into smaller units.

- Start working on the first unit. Give yourself rewards as you progress—a break, a cup of coffee, note the progress on a chart.
- Save for the end some of the more pleasurable tasks that can be postponed.

"IN DELAY THERE LIES NO PLENTY"
(SHAKESPEARE)

37. Stop for a while When you are running out of ideas or energy for a task, or there's a puzzle you can't seem to solve, stop for a while. It's remarkable how solutions appear when you return to a task refreshed.

"TIME COOLS, TIME CLARIFIES;"
(THOMAS MANN)

38. Unpleasant task Do not wait until the last day and the last hour to do unpleasant or difficult tasks.

- The postponed task looms over you and grows more aversive as time passes.
- You will be under stress when you try to complete it at the last moment.
- You may rush through it or even fail to finish on time.

"TIME GOES, YOU SAY? AH NO! ALAS, TIME STAYS, WE GO.
(HENRY DOBSON).

39. Write it now Clutter is your enemy; lists are your friends.

TIME-SAVING TIP

INFLUENCE

FOCUS

Make it a habit to jot your thoughts down, so your mind isn't cluttered with a dozen projects and appointments. Put tasks and notes about them on To-Do lists; put deadlines, appointments and reminders in your calendar; make entries in computer files or in folders.

DOUBLING UP

40. Activities Since you never know when you may be obliged to wait away from your home and office, it's prudent to carry a few things with you to make the most of that time:

- reading material
- a highlight marker
- pen and pencil
- writing paper or a palmtop computer or memo recorder
- your calendar and a printout of tasks—or your palmtop

41. Concurrent activities Ways to double up and be (almost) twice as productive:

- Do routine desk work while on hold with speakerphone set.
- Send and receive telephone messages while driving.
- Think about projects while showering, grooming.
- Listen to prerecorded tapes, CDs while driving.
- Place phone calls while printing out documents, email.
- Work with a laptop in planes and trains.
- Read professional material while on vacation.
- Read catalogs, bulletins, newsletters in the toilet. Or at the hair stylist. Or on an exercise bike, treadmill, or other stationary fitness machine.
- Bike to work, or find another way to combine exercise and commuting.

42. Deadlines It is wise to assign a deadline to every project; otherwise it is difficult to set priorities.

When accepting a task, always negotiate the deadline in the light of your other commitments.

"TIME TAKES ALL AND GIVES ALL."
(GIORDANO BRUNO)

43. Discoveries

When you are away from home or the office and have some time to spare, you may be able to run errands that will save you time later on.

- Are there greeting cards, gifts, toiletries or items of clothing you've been meaning to pick up?
- Are there restaurants or athletic facilities you'd like to check out?

"TIME IS MAN'S ANGEL."
(JOHANN VON SCHILLER)

44. Home

"HOLD FAST THE TIME! GUARD IT, WATCH OVER IT,
EVERY HOUR, EVERY MINUTE!
UNREGARDED IT SLIPS AWAY, LIKE A LIZARD."
(THOMAS MANN).

Take advantage of the scraps of time that appear between activities:

- Five minutes. Have five minutes before your next appointment or activity? Here are a few things you can do to use the time: Return a (short) phone call; make an appointment; write a note; straighten your desk (room, etc.); pay a bill; scan To-Do list; stretch.
- Ten minutes. Sort some mail; take a catnap; make a phone call; write a brief letter on a computer; scan a magazine article.
- Thirty minutes. Skim a report; work on writing one; sort through periodicals; pay some bills; balance your checkbook; enter data in a file; reorganize a closet; send out notes or other brief correspondence; catch up on phone calls.

TIME-SAVING TIP   INFLUENCE   FOCUS

45. Learning from mistakes A mishap can be more valuable at times than faultless execution, for the mishap may signal a disaster lying in wait or an opportunity that has been neglected. Therefore, do not view a mishap only as a setback; the thing to focus on is what caused it. Once you know that, you can take remedial action. Whether it be a missed appointment, a tumble down the stairs at home, or some misunderstood instructions, the mishap is an opportunity you pass up at your own risk.

"HE THAT WILL NOT APPLY NEW REMEDIES MUST EXPECT NEW EVILS; FOR TIME IS THE GREATEST INNOVATOR."

(FRANCIS BACON)

46. Monitoring progress Getting the job done right and on time requires monitoring progress and taking corrective action as necessary.

- Monitor progress on your own work. Put sub-goals in your calendar. True, it's unpleasant to arrive at the first sub-goal and recognize that at that rate you will never finish on time—but there is still time for corrective action.
- Monitor progress on projects you assign to others. Ask them to fill you in at agreed upon dates.

47. While waiting in line Once in a rare while, you cannot avoid waiting in line unless you are ready to forgo the event, and you are not.

- Ask the person next to you in line if they would like you to hold their place while they get some coffee or run an errand. If they decline, ask them if they mind holding your place while you do the same.
- Bring along a friend or family member with whom you have been planning to spend time.
- Bring a book, some papers you need to examine, a pad to write on, or a list of calls to make with your cellular phone. One good topic for reflection: what slip-ups led me to wait on this line?

 BENEFITS   BURDENS   BALANCE   **General Strategies for Saving Time**

GET ORGANIZED

⏱ **48. Analyze the problem** Business communications pioneer Dale Carnegie claims that answering the following questions can reduce by half the time spent on a problem.

1. What is the problem?
2. What is the cause of the problem?
3. What are all the possible solutions to the problem?
4. What is the best solution?

⏱ **49. General principles** Get-organized wizard Emilie Barnes advises:

- Don't put it down, put it away.
- Store like things together.
- Write it down, and read it.
- Invest in proper tools.
- Use labels and signs.
- Delegate to your family and others.
- Get rid of things you don't use.
- Use master lists.

⏱ **50. Over-organized** Are you over-organized? Yes: You almost never look for documents. You may have a filing system that is too elaborate, requiring too much time for storage.

No: You frequently spend time looking. You have a simple filing system, fast on storage but slow on retrieval.

The goal is to choose a level of organization that strikes a balance between the time it takes for storing information and for retrieving it.

⏱ **51. Quiet hour** Try to schedule a "quiet hour" into your day, a time at work or at home when interruptions are discouraged: put a sign on the door, shut off the phone. This is your chance to immerse yourself in a project, to think deeply about it. (You may also want to take a break or a nap, or review progress toward current goals.)

⏱

TIME-SAVING TIP　　INFLUENCE　　FOCUS

Surveys show that one uninterrupted hour is worth three normal hours of productivity.

52. Seek paradigms Avoid specialized solutions. Build a paradigm as you solve the problem the first time. If you make it general, you can apply it to new cases efficiently.

> EXAMPLE: You are short on time to shop for food. You could try to squeeze it in or ask a friend for a favor, but you prefer to try a new Internet shopping service in your city. It will take a while the first time—setting up an account, listing your selections—but thereafter you can repeat the order in a flash.

53. Urgent or important? Urgent doesn't mean important. The pressure of urgent tasks distorts priorities. Keep focused on the tasks that are important and set aside time for them daily before they become urgent.

GOALS

54. Cop-outs

It is easy to mistake activity for results.

"I called them but they were out," or "I spend an hour a day on it" are about activities.

"I gave him the message," and "I am halfway through the revisions" are about results.

Express your goals in measurable results not in activities, set dates for achieving those goals; identify sub-goals and the activities that should accomplish them.

55. Focus Achieving goals is not only about discipline or will, it's about arranging circumstances to support your efforts.

> EXAMPLE: You decide to have an uncluttered desk. You purchase trays to hold the various types of documents (see Business-Office-Clutter),

establish a filing system (Business-Office-Filing), set aside a few minutes in your calendar each morning to sort incoming mail and review pending projects.

 56. Insight You can save a great deal of time by understanding your own motivation. If, for lack of that understanding, you accept or stay with the wrong job, make the wrong friends, marry the wrong person, choose the wrong vacation spot, and so on, the cost in time is breathtaking.

All behavior makes sense. If you have identified some of your long-term goals and observe that you are not acting in accord with them, try to identify the forces at work:

- What short-term rewards or fears are keeping you at the unproductive activity? How could they be changed?
- How can you instate productive activities that will crowd out the unproductive ones?
- Unproductive activity was often productive at one time and then conditions changed. To gain insight into that process, trained professionals like psychologists and psychiatrists can help; so can friends and support groups.

> "A MAN ALWAYS HAS TWO REASONS FOR WHAT HE DOES—A
> GOOD ONE, AND THE REAL ONE."
>
> (J. PIERPONT MORGAN)

 57. Motto
WRITE IT! READ IT! DO IT! is our motto.

- In light of your goals, WRITE a to-do list of tasks.
- As additional steps occur to you, WRITE them down.
- READ your list from time to time and cross out tasks accomplished.
- Pick some tasks that remain in view of their priority and the time you have available and DO them.

58. Personal development Want to make progress toward personal and professional goals? Draw up a list of those goals (personal or professional development, health, home life, social relations . . .) and answer these questions:

 TIME-SAVING TIP   INFLUENCE   FOCUS

- Are these the goals I am deeply committed to pursuing?
- Is the set of goals consistent? Will some activities serve several goals? (Example: joining a gym can be social as well as athletic.)
- Are the goals realistic for me? Can I make significant progress toward them in a reasonable period of time?
- What resources, human and material, will I need to make progress? Are these reasonably available to me?
- How can I measure my progress and the outcome?
- What are some of the rewards along the way that will sustain my motivation?

59. Priorities The opposite of wasting time is spending it on your priorities. To know if you are managing your time wisely:

- Identify some of your priorities.
- Estimate how much time you are devoting to them.
- Assess whether that time is productive. Try this "suppose": Suppose you were going to leave this earth in good health six months from today. What would you want to be sure to have done and experienced before your time is up? Interesting. Maybe you should give those a little more priority. If some of the things you really want to do are getting shortchanged by the busyness of life, take steps!
- Schedule the want-to-do in your calendar.
- Undertake the activity with other people, so it will be harder to skip.
- Sign up and pay a fee, if appropriate.
- Make your new commitment public.
- Remove or reduce other activities to make time for this one.

60. Rewards Plan rewards for completing tasks.

EXAMPLE: instead of having one more cup of coffee before you start returning "all those calls," return the calls and then reward yourself with a cup of coffee.

When you complete larger projects, promise yourself a fine meal, a movie you've been wanting to see, a trip to the country . . .

BENEFITS

BURDENS

BALANCE

61. Shared goals In a couple, individual activities can sometimes lead the partners in opposite directions.

Identify some shared goals: join a club or reading group together; go skiing; travel; redecorate; get organized; have your palms read.

INTERPERSONAL

62. Ask for help

When starting a new task, you can save time if you:

- Ask for tips from friends and coworkers.
- Set aside time to brainstorm with them.
- Consult standard information sources.
- Ask your local reference librarian for information.
- Search the Web.

63. Blame If you are busy blaming someone for a task done poorly or not at all, you are probably not engaged in a cool-headed analysis of how the problem arose, and your part in it.

- Did you assign the task wisely?
- Were your instructions clear?
- Did you set a reasonable time for completion?
- Did you monitor and reward progress?

64. Friendship More than the people of many nations, Americans relocate. This makes it especially hard to keep friendships current. If that is a priority in your life, here are some steps you can take:

- Dash off an email.
- Make a phone call: ("I was just thinking of you . . . ").
- Send them a greeting card.
- Propose that you visit them.
- Propose that they visit you.

 TIME-SAVING TIP   INFLUENCE   FOCUS

- Vacation together.
- Consider a collaboration in some area.

> "A MAN SHOULD KEEP HIS FRIENDSHIPS
> IN A CONSTANT REPAIR."
> (SAMUEL JOHNSON)

65. Getting the decision you want When people fail to make the decision you need, it can take up a lot of your time—continuing to press for it, looking elsewhere, managing without it. Here's a three-step solution.

GET TO THE DECISION-MAKER (DM).
- Identify who can make the decision you want.
- Like the king in chess, the DM has pawns out in front to stop you. Ask pleasantly but insistently to speak with the DM.
- Explain why he or she will want to speak with you.
- Ask for a telephone appointment with the DM; do not accept a promise of a call back.
- If you are getting nowhere, ask for the names of the pawn and his or her supervisor and ask to speak with the supervisor.
- Send the DM a fax; then, when you call, say that you are following up on communications with the DM.
- Call the national headquarters, ask the operator for the secretary of the vice-president for sales, public relations, etc., and explain why you and the DM need to speak.
- "Network." Do you know someone who knows someone who can put in a word for you with the DM?

MAKE YOUR CASE TO THE DECISION-MAKER.
- State clearly and briefly just what you want, why it is appropriate, and how the interests of the DM will be served by it.
- Break the larger decision down into smaller ones that are easier for the DM to make: May I send you some documents to read? Then: When can we meet to discuss this further? Then: Would you like to meet with X, Y and Z or visit P?

BENEFITS

BURDENS

BALANCE

- Suggest some dates for these events; don't leave them open-ended.
- Listen to the DM's response. What is he or she saying? What's their larger point, their feelings? Speak little (if you're "making a pitch," it's suspicious) but ask questions that clarify the issues. What are your basic disagreements that stand in the way of a "yes"? Can they be reduced to just one or two issues?

BUILD TRUST.
- Anticipate the DM's objections. State the concern, and how you will deal with it.
- Read up on the DM, their company or agency.
- Be friendly. Even if you're mad enough to spit nails, keep smiling or you'll get the other person's back up.
- Dress conservatively (like the bankers to whom we entrust our money). Be well groomed.
- Arrive on time.
- Bring everything relevant.
- Make statements the DM believes are true.
- Acknowledge the legitimacy of what the DM says whenever possible.
- Summarize the pros and cons in a way that appears to be fair yet shows a net advantage to the decision you are seeking. Give the DM a clear overview—through your rose-colored glasses.

✸ 66. Humor Humor establishes a positive relationship early.

EXAMPLE: **At the hardware store, "Did you ever meet a man with all thumbs? Well, I need . . . "**

"HUMOR SAVES A FEW STEPS, IT SAVES YEARS."
(MARIANNE MOORE)

✸ 67. Influence
- Analyze the broad goal into sub-goals.
- Identify the activities that must be carried out to achieve each of those sub-goals.

 TIME-SAVING TIP   INFLUENCE   FOCUS

- Identify rewards that will be meted out as progress is made.

EXAMPLE: Teaching a teenager to pass a driving test. Both factual knowledge and skills must be taught.

Skills. Steering at low speed in a large empty parking lot might be a place to begin.

Rewards. Potential rewards include approval at the first successful maneuvers, acknowledgment in front of the family, perhaps release from a chore or the gift of a desired excursion. When steering has been mastered, what logically comes next?

68. Long-term relations Long-term relations take a lot of time. Sweethearts require wooing, calling, dating, and bedding; spouses generally take even more time. Children require cleaning, feeding, dressing, instructing, and surveillance just for openers.

Don't take on a long-term relation without first reviewing your personal and professional goals. How many long-term relations are compatible with those goals? True, some Frenchmen have professions, wives, children, pets, AND mistresses but this is a bravura performance in time management you may not be able to equal in the U.S.

Life's sweetest moments and greatest opportunities for personal growth and service to others come from long-term relations. Time saving is not an end in itself; rather it should allow us to be better parents, children, spouses and partners, friends and collaborators.

69. Loyalty When you are a loyal patron of a restaurant, shop, gas station, travel agent, etc., make it known. Write down a few key names and develop friendly relations with those persons. You will enjoy your patronage more and you will receive better service in the long-run. For the same reasons, stick with the same merchants if you are convinced of their quality.

70. Make a note
When I see X, I must tell her Y.

BENEFITS   BURDENS   BALANCE

- Why wait? Call or send an email and be done with it.
- Or make a note of it in your tickler file or calendar.

71. Praise plus
Reward the people with whom you work when they are moving in the direction of better time management.

- Thank them for meeting deadlines; tell them how it helped.
- Praise the quality of their work when it is deserved.
- Back up thanks and praise with more substantial rewards like raises and promotions.

72. Providing feedback
Someone is wasting your time:

- Tell them; they may not know it. And explain why it is a problem for you. (Example: When you arrive late, you make me late for my next appointment.)
- Acknowledge their many good points (I certainly value your advice . . .).
- Help them to analyze the problem (Would it help if we met at a different time?).
- Is there anything YOU could have done to avoid the problem?

73. Reverse brainstorming
To improve a technique or a project, list everything wrong with it. Then take each wrong thing and brainstorm ways to overcome it.

74. Saving the employee's time
Time wasted for salespeople and professionals is income lost. They will be more respectful of your time if you show that you value theirs.

- Bring the information with you that you need in order to select items or services—the space that the dishwasher must fit in; the part that attaches to the part you need to replace; your calendar to book appointments.
- Prepare a list of features you want in your selection by reading up (in Consumer Reports, on the Web, etc.) and talking with family, friends and neighbors.

 TIME-SAVING TIP   INFLUENCE FOCUS

- Carry with you a note of your measurements and those of others for whom you are likely to buy clothing.

75. Services

When you show people consideration, you can trust their ingenuity to solve problems. "I can't do it" will become "I'm not sure I can do it," then "I'll see what I can do" and, finally, "I'll find a way to do it." Example: you call an electrician.

- Greet him or her, offer them some coffee.
- Describe the problem and ask how they size it up.
- Point out where the phone and bathroom are, should they need to use them.
- The promise of an appropriate tip may help.
- Show that you understand their feelings ("You're working late").
- Show that you respect their expertise ("I need your advice").

76. Socializing

Socializing on the job can waste time but it can also advance your agenda since good relations are important and you may gather helpful information through informal conversation.

77. Soliciting feedback

Consider soliciting feedback from others concerning your time management. Ask your spouse, child, coworker, friend whether you are supportive of their efforts at managing their time.

You may find out that you are often later than you realized, or ask for help at the last moment, or leave others unclear about deadlines . . .

78. Work and home

If your work and your home are in different locations, relations with co-workers are best addressed at work, relations with family and friends at home—except for emergencies, of course. If you work at home, consider allocating certain hours to work exclusively, other hours to your personal life.

BENEFITS

BURDENS

BALANCE

79. Work with a friend Plan collaboration on a project with a friend: It can be more enjoyable, innovative, and productive and you will be less likely to procrastinate.

LISTS

80. Checklists In this book, you will find numerous checklists, including the following: Office Supplies (Tip 188), Shopping (386), Parties (420), Appliances and Utensils (536), Tools (575), Home Filing (591), Supplies (607), What to Have in Your Car (665), Packing (675), Flights (688), and Business Trips (700).

81. Importance Lists are a highly effective form of "trap yourself"—a method of controlling your own behavior.

- A list of tasks often has a logical order; the right order saves you time, effort and money.
- With a list, you can set priorities, so that the most important work is more certain of your attention.
- Crossing completed tasks off a list is self-reinforcement that helps you move toward your goal.
- Written down tasks are unlikely to be overlooked. Forget your worry that something significant will be neglected.
- But when situations change, when insights arise, revise your list. With computer software for maintaining to-do lists, you can easily move items about, add some and delete others, assign priorities and receive reminders at planned dates and times.
- The list must not be a cop-out. Writing a task down is not even a little like accomplishing it. You actually have to use the list.
- Your tray of current projects may serve as a kind of list provided you scan through the contents frequently (like scanning your list), that there is a piece of paper (letter, document, note, whatever) for every task, and that you keep the content and ordering of the tray up to date.

TIME-SAVING TIP

INFLUENCE

FOCUS

82. Loans It's so annoying to look everywhere for a book, record or tool that you have lent to someone else.

Make a list (in your computer or in a folder) of such loans, with the dates and the borrowers' names. You might make a note in your calendar at a later date to check if the loan was returned.

83. Master list Personal Information Manager (PIM) software allows you to keep your To-Do list of tasks alongside your calendar, to set target dates for tasks, and to group tasks into projects and assign priorities.

- Keep a master To-Do list and a daily list. It is simplest and safest to carry the master list with you and make additions to it directly.
- Review your To-Do list as you start your day. Which things must be done today? What longer-term projects can you also work on today? Do you need to block time on your calendar to accomplish them?
- As you complete tasks, cross them off your master list. From time to time consolidate and reorganize the list.

84. Personal projects Keep lists in your computer or on paper that will assist you in personal activities: Movies and shows you would like to see or rent; books you want to borrow or buy; vacation ideas and contacts; restaurant recommendations; friends you want to invite or visit; gifts you have received and those you have given; gifts you plan to buy for friends and relatives; Christmas cards you have received and sent.

85. Pocket reminder How do you handle important reminders?

A computerized calendar will prompt you, but you have to be within earshot. Ask your secretary, spouse or friend to remind you but you may not be easy to reach in time (unless you have a cell phone or pager).

Write the item on a piece of paper and put it in your pocket along with your keys. When you reach for those keys, you're bound to come across the slip of paper.

BENEFITS

BURDENS

BALANCE

86. Priorities You have scanned your master To-Do list and have picked out some things to work on during the day. But what are your priorities?

You might use the Michelin method of rating restaurants—stars. Put three stars next to your top priorities, two stars next to important but lesser activities, and one star for nice to get to but can be postponed.

Ask yourself: If I had to reduce my workday, which projects would I set aside?

87. Questions Prepare for events with ordered lists.

- A medical checkup? You may have questions for your doctor you don't want to forget.
- A meeting with your boss: projects to review.
- A visit from a contractor: repairs that are needed.

88. Reminders If you are afraid of forgetting something the next morning (e.g., to fast for your medical checkup) write it on a Post-it and stick it on the bathroom mirror. You can also put things on top of the purse, attaché case or briefcase that you carry.

89. Time/Date Put the date and time on all your lists and notes. Most software will do it automatically.

 TIME-SAVING TIP   INFLUENCE   FOCUS

SAYING NO

90. Declining gracefully

"YOU CAN ASK ME FOR ANYTHING YOU LIKE, EXCEPT TIME."
(NAPOLEON)

"NO!" is a terrific time-saving tool.

If you said "no" more often, you would have more time but, good-natured soul that you are, you hate to disappoint the other person. The solution:

- Say "no." Be firm but friendly.
- Say why. Your other tasks will suffer. Your tax auditor has moved in with you. You're not the best person for the task.
- Say something constructive. Who is the best person for the task? Can the task be redefined?

EXAMPLE: THE PROFESSOR SAID "NO"
- to a student's request for a letter of reference (it would weaken her application to have a letter from someone who didn't know her work well; weren't there others who did?).
- to a scholar's request to read her manuscript (I was not expert enough to be of real value but X and Y are).
- to a talk show (a member of the constituency concerned, such as Mr. Z, would be a better spokesperson).
- to a government agency (my evaluation of their proposal could not be done thoroughly before their deadline but P or Q might be able to help).

91. Do it now

When you know you must say no, say it. If you postpone, you may lead the other person on for a while and also waste your time dealing with them on this issue.

"MY UNHAPPINESS WAS THE UNHAPPINESS OF A PERSON
WHO COULD NOT SAY NO."
(DAZAI OSAMU)

BENEFITS   BURDENS   BALANCE

92. Information overload

Focus on saying no to needless information:

- You do not need to process all the information that comes your way. Try to screen out unnecessary information, using a minimum of effort and attention.
- Don't sign up to be a recipient in the first place unless it is important (too many magazines, too many memos).
- If you are receiving some information but do not need it, discontinue it.
- As needless information comes into your house or onto your desk, toss it out.
- End phone calls from solicitors promptly with "Sorry, not interested."
- Ask to be removed from email distribution lists.
- If you are part of a group that regularly produces documents, challenge the need. Is every one of the reports you receive from subordinates necessary? Could a few be combined into one with less periodicity? Request that documents start with an executive summary and are brief. Check on whether addressees really use the document.
- When registering a product, you are often given the option to decline mailings from the manufacturer and from its business partners. Decline.

93. Saying no to yourself

You are good at saying no to others, but can you say no to yourself?

You are often the instigator for social events, personal development and fitness activities and family events. Have you taken too many on?

Make a list of those activities: what are their priorities? Should any of them be discontinued or suspended?

"TO THINK IS TO SAY NO."
(EMILE CHARTIER)

94. Stop (time) thief!

Time management analyst Alec MacKenzie asked many managers to identify the major time thieves in their lives. They were of two sorts — "their fault" and "my fault," though we think they largely boil down to a failure to

TIME-SAVING TIP

INFLUENCE

FOCUS

use two important strategies: Saying no (See Strategies—Saying no) and Delegating (See Strategies—Delegating).

EXTERNAL TIME THIEVES:
- needless or needlessly long telephone calls
- interruptions by collaborators
- our open-door policy
- unscheduled meetings with visitors or clients
- incompetent assistants
- my boss or, worse, bosses
- business meals
- unnecessary meetings
- meetings too frequent, long or ill-prepared
- managing family affairs
- home and home furnishings maintenance
- taking children to appointments
- shopping, cleaning, cooking
- interruptions by my children or my parents

INTERNAL TIME THIEVES
- unclear and changing goals and priorities
- lack of a daily plan
- unfinished business
- failure to impose deadlines on myself
- my perfectionism
- my disorderly habits
- unclear lines of responsibility
- insufficient delegating
- delay in resolving conflicts
- resistance to change
- lack of information
- indecisiveness or hasty decisions
- stress and fatigue

BENEFITS

BURDENS

BALANCE

SCHEDULE CONTROL

🕐 **95. Allow more time** If you need an estimated two weeks to do something, consider allowing three. You are more certain to meet the deadline and will feel less stressed along the way. Besides, most people underestimate the time required.

If you are going on a three-day trip, block off four days on your calendar. Use the extra day to settle back in, catch up on the paperwork accumulated in your absence, and work on longer term projects if there's time left over.

🕐 **96. As soon as possible** Just as there is "security creep" in classified papers (increasingly the lowest levels of protection are not used), so there is deadline creep in projects. What is really needed in a week is said to be needed ASAP.

Whenever you undertake a project—from painting the kitchen to writing a report— negotiate a realistic deadline; refuse ASAP. If it really must be done today, then today is the deadline; if not, when is it needed by?

🕐 **97. Booking times**
Use your calendar for more than just appointments.

- Schedule time to work on your goals and sub goals;
- time in anticipation of deadlines;
- time for activities that otherwise might be crowded out, like planning, evaluating, building interpersonal relations, career development, making progress on health and fitness goals.

"TO EVERY THING THERE IS A SEASON, AND A TIME TO EVERY PURPOSE UNDER THE HEAVEN."
(ECCLESIASTES 3:1-8)

98. Breaks Depending on your workload, allow yourself a period of time (an hour daily, or an hour weekly) without any planned activity or appointments.

 TIME-SAVING TIP   INFLUENCE   FOCUS

Use that hour to take a break, go for a walk, think long thoughts, or review your personal development, health and social goals and activities (those are the ones that often are neglected).

99. Breaks Working long and intensely is not always productive: after a while, the volume and quality of your work can be impaired. Program some breaks into your schedule, say ten minutes every hour or so. Use the break to reward yourself for completing a section or unit.

100. Calendar Among printed calendars, we prefer large ones that have enough space for daily events but allow you to see your week at a glance.

Computerized calendars have advantages: single entry for repeated appointments; good searching; easy revisions. And disadvantages: You must print the calendar out repeatedly in order to carry an updated version with you—unless you have a palmtop computer (See Computers—Hardware—Palmtops).

"A CALENDAR! A CALENDAR!"

(SHAKESPEARE)

101. Calendar use

Look at your calendar at the start of the work day, to answer these questions:

- What preparation does each appointment require?
- How can I move appointments to free up blocks of time?
- What are the priority tasks to accomplish today?
- What are the email and mail messages I want to respond to today?

Look at your calendar at the end of the workday to answer these questions:

- What tasks for today must be moved to tomorrow or later?
- What work should I take home (if any)?

BENEFITS

BURDENS

BALANCE

Look at your calendar at bedtime:

- Place needed papers or diskettes in your briefcase.
- Lay out clothes for the morning.

102. Calm moments Many people like to arrive early at their office to enjoy the calm; others stay late for the same reason. Best not to do both regularly.

With some planning you can create periods of calm during the work day:

- Hang a Do Not Disturb sign on your door and use it.
- Punch the Do Not Disturb button on your phone.

103. Flexibility

Consider moving recurring activities around in your schedule.

EXAMPLE: People keep disturbing you at the start of the workday while you are reading your mail. Consider setting aside time for that a little later in the day.

104. Leave more time From the stressful dash to work that starts your day, to the dash home that ends it, consider leaving more time to get places.

You leave late for appointments because:

- You don't want to waste time arriving early. Bring work with you (a book to read, correspondence . . .); if there is time to spare, you can make good use of it.
- You get caught up in what you are doing. Have a person or device (for example, your computerized calendar) remind you.

105. Log Keep a log for a few days, recording the start and end time of all your activities, including wash-up, breakfast, commute, etc.

Now examine the list in relation to your goals. Are there goals you are neglecting? Are you losing valuable time in low priority activities?

TIME-SAVING TIP INFLUENCE FOCUS

106. Meetings To avoid going beyond the time you had allotted for a meeting, ask someone to call you on the phone or to interrupt with a reminder.

107. Punctuality Leave early enough to be on time at work, at an appointment or at home and expect others to do so.

Except for acts of God (as insurance policies say) there's no valid excuse: we all know that traffic fluctuates, that parking is hell, that trains arrive late, etc.

Err on the early side but bring work with you in case you arrive in advance.

108. Surprises Block off some time each day for the unexpected. You may need that time for a family matter, an urgent request, a last-minute appointment, an unplanned act of kindness, or you may use it to work on a priority project.

109. Time management

"TIME IS THE VERY SOUL OF THIS WORLD."
(PYTHAGORAS)

Focus on Basic Time-Management Steps

- Identify Goals. Time can be managed well or badly only in relation to some purpose. Therefore, identify your major goals and sub-goals and some activities that follow from them.

EXAMPLE **Goal: Fit recreation into my life. Sub-goal: club membership. Activities, visit two fitness centers near me; check with X on joint membership; sign up.**

- Set Priorities. First priority goes to activities that are both important (they move you toward important goals) and urgent. Lowest priority goes to activities that are neither.

BENEFITS
BURDENS
BALANCE

General Strategies for Saving Time

The catch: Important but not urgent tasks tend to pile up until they, too, become urgent. Raise their priority early on to avoid that.

- Conduct self-assessment. Does your current schedule match your priorities? Keep a fairly detailed calendar for a week or two, then add up the periods of time associated with related activities like sleeping, commuting, entertainment, meetings, etc.
- Make a schedule. Advance scheduling is the best way to insure that you spend time on your priorities. Identify who should carry out each activity; estimate the time required; choose a day and time for each in view of your priorities and enter it in your calendar. At the end of each week, adjust the schedule for the following week.
- Follow-up. Repeat self-assessment. Does your schedule match your priorities better? Which low priority activities are taking too much time?

110. Waiting Don't wait for anyone who won't wait for you. People who commonly make you wait are professional people. Tell them candidly you don't have the time to spare. Tell their appointments secretary that you, like their boss, are tightly scheduled and want an appointment when he or she is most likely to be on time, so that you can stay on time.

As a rule of thumb wait fifteen minutes but no more; your friends and colleagues will learn to respect that.

> "FOR TO LOSE TIME IS MOST DISPLEASING
> TO HIM WHO KNOWS MOST."
> (DANTE ALIGHIERI)

111. Welcome change
An unexpected change in your routine can be an opportunity to find new ways to save time—if you are on the lookout.

EXAMPLE: your secretary is out for the day and you try composing letters with your PC rather than with a Dictaphone; you find you prefer the PC and it takes only slightly longer.

TIME-SAVING TIP

INFLUENCE

FOCUS

EXAMPLE: Your commuting route home is blocked; you try another and discover a shopping center that has a useful constellation of shops for your needs.

"CHANCE IS A NICKNAME FOR PROVIDENCE."
(SÉBASTIEN CHAMFORT)

SELF-MANAGEMENT

112. Deadlines Many busy people set their watches a little fast, to give themselves some leeway in arriving at appointments on time.

Similarly, if you have a task to be completed by a certain day, put an earlier deadline on your list or calendar that will leave you a little leeway if something comes up or if you underestimated the time the task required.

If it looks like you will not be able to meet a deadline, notify the other party in advance; this gives them more leeway for remedial action.

113. Find a friend If your goals in personal development, health and social activities are being neglected, consider making a regular appointment for certain activities with a family member or friend. The event may be more pleasant and it will be harder for you to cancel it at the last moment.

Helps you stick to your schedule for sports or other interests.

Find the right friend, find the time.

114. Prompting To increase the chances you will engage in the activities your goals call for, prompt yourself.

- Plan your time allocation for the week on Sunday and keep the plan visible during the week; your plan will prompt you.

- Program your computerized calendar to pop up a notice and ring a bell to prompt you.
- Put the project you really should work on on top of the stack and it will prompt you.
- Keep a visible chart of how much time you are spending on a desired (or undesired) activity, and the chart will prompt you.
- Prompt yourself by putting tools for the desired activity—clothes for the gym, books for the project, a wrench for the home repair—in conspicuous locations.
- Photocopy tips and strategies in this book that particularly speak to your situation, enlarge them and post them where they will prompt you.

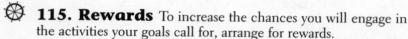 **115. Rewards** To increase the chances you will engage in the activities your goals call for, arrange for rewards.

You know you must provide rewards; you express your appreciation, give public recognition, pay money—and yet you don't apply the same principle to yourself. What are you, inhuman?

The rewards you schedule for yourself must be contingent on the desired behavior—that is, no activity, no reward—and they should promptly follow the desired behavior.

EXAMPLE: Free-lance professionals reward themselves for a productive few hours' work by taking some time off.

Make an informal contract with yourself—when I finish this letter, I'll call home—or you may contract with others: If I can get this project done by the weekend, I'll join you skiing.

You can help the people you care about achieve their goals by rewarding them, and you can ask their help in supporting you by making a point of providing you with rewards as appropriate when you carry out the desired activities.

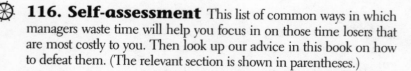 **116. Self-assessment** This list of common ways in which managers waste time will help you focus in on those time losers that are most costly to you. Then look up our advice in this book on how to defeat them. (The relevant section is shown in parentheses.)

Communication, ineffective (Strategies-Interpersonal)
Crises (Strategies-Do It Now)

 TIME-SAVING TIP   INFLUENCE   FOCUS

Deadlines, unrealistic (Strategies-Schedule Control)
Delegation, infrequent or ineffective (Strategies-Delegating)
Goals & sub-goals poorly defined (Strategies-Goals)
Interruptions (Business-Office-Interruptions; Strategies-Get Organized-Interruptions)
Listening, failure of (Strategies-Interpersonal)
Meetings (Business-Appointments; Social-Meetings)
Organization, lack of (Strategies-Get Organized)
Priorities, failure to set (Strategies-Sequencing Tasks)
Procrastination (Strategies-Procrastination)
Routine tasks (Strategies-Schedule Control)
Say No, inability to (Strategies-Saying No)
Socializing, idle (Strategies-Schedule Control)
Task completion, difficulty with (Strategies-Procrastination)
Task scheduling, failure of (Strategies-Schedule Control)
Telephone calls (Communication-Telephone)
Travel & commuting (Travel)

"MISSPENDING A MAN'S TIME IS A KIND OF SELF-HOMICIDE."
(GEORGE SAVILLE)

117. Setting milestones Think of sub-goals as milestones; reward yourself when you reach them.

EXAMPLE: **Health goal—Fitness.**

- One-year goals: 12 pounds less, 30 min aerobic activity and 5 min stretching 3 times weekly.
- Monthly sub-goals: 1 pound less, 3 min more aerobic activity, ½ min more stretching.

Check yourself monthly; collect your reward or, if you fell short, identify causes and revise sub-goals.

EXAMPLE: **Career goal—Writing.**

Psychologist B.F. Skinner kept a daily record of the time he spent writing. Each evening, he added the time spent to the running total and plotted a point on a graph showing the total time and the corresponding date.

Skinner could see readily when he was increasing his efforts

BENEFITS   BURDENS   BALANCE   **General Strategies for Saving Time**   43

(the plot curved upward) and when he was slacking off (it curved down).

Most of all, he took pleasure in seeing the line inch upward toward his goal of chapter completion. Writers Ernest Hemingway and Irving Wallace did something similar.

👍 Helps to keep you motivated when the major reward is a long way off.

👎 Time to analyze long-term goals into sub-goals and to monitor progress.

⚙ **118. Warming up** You have blocked off time in your schedule for this project and now that time has come. You delayed a few minutes clearing your desktop, clipping a hangnail, and re-arranging some pens and pencils. Now there is just you and a pad of paper (or PC screen) and the moment that all creative people dread has arrived.

Don't try and leap the hurdle from a dead start—run up to it! Plan to look at materials that will prompt you, thus bringing the right vocabulary and concepts more readily to mind.

Then, create an outline to prompt you. List the main points (surely less than a dozen). Re-order the list so it follows logically. Then list the secondary points under each main point and put them in the right order. Finally, list and order tertiary points if necessary. With a detailed outline, writing consists largely of putting the outline phrases into complete sentences and writing transitional sentences. Other valuable prompts are diagrams, charts and the like—post them directly in your line of sight several days in advance of when you need to write about them.

SEQUENCING TASKS

🕐 **119. Clusters** Cluster calls and other small tasks so the large and difficult ones receive uninterrupted attention.

 TIME-SAVING TIP   INFLUENCE   FOCUS

120. Concurrency Maximize concurrency.

> EXAMPLE: You need to write a long letter and to order a book; if you place the order first, chances are the book will arrive sooner than if you write the letter first.

121. Lists Concurrency: Whenever you leave the house, ask yourself what errands can be conveniently included in your routing. Carry with you a list of special purchases to make.
Avoid multiple trips.

122. Segments Break large tasks into shorter segments so that you can work on them when you find a short period free.

TIME IS MONEY

123. Calculate its value Compute how much one hour of your time is worth. This will allow you to see the value in dollars of time-saving steps that you take.
If you can earn money during the saved time, you can estimate your additional income and compute the "payback" of time-saving moves that require an investment. Here's a rule of thumb to help you calculate the value of your time based on your salary: Your time is worth $6.70 an hour for every $10,000 of salary you earn. For example, if you earn $25,000 annually, your time is worth $16.75/hr. (This includes a 40% provision for benefits you receive such as retirement and health insurance).

124. Cheaper stores When you estimate how much you save by driving to a remote place to shop, remember to deduct the cost of gas and the dollar value of your time.

125. Complaints If you have a problem with a company and you can't solve it with them, call the state Attorney General's

BENEFITS

BURDENS

BALANCE

office of consumer complaints, or the Better Business Bureau, or the appropriate regulatory agency such as the state Banking Commission, the state Commissioner of Utilities, the Federal Aviation Authority, etc.

126. Freed-up time It can save you money to free up some of your time by hiring others to do the work. Many workers can elect to work overtime; many self-employed people can earn more income if they put in more hours; a teacher with more discretionary time might write a textbook, a salesman cover more territory, and so forth.

Conversely, if you are already working overtime and find work crowding out some of your priorities, you may want to spend less money in some areas which will allow you to cut back on overtime.

WAITING

127. Don't go there

"I WASTED TIME, AND NOW DOTH TIME WASTE ME."
(SHAKESPEARE)

There are many places you should never (or very rarely) go if you value your time. City Hall. A post office. A department store. The bank. (See Strategies—Waiting—Reducing Waiting)

- In general, when someone tells you to go to a place to transact some business, alarm bells should ring. Tell the person, or their supervisor, that "it's not possible for me to come down. Is there some way we can do this by mail, email, courier or fax?" Cordial resistance can spare you countless trips and waiting in line.

128. Lines Don't wait in line. If you're waiting in line you are doing something wrong: you'll find throughout this book, and

TIME-SAVING TIP

INFLUENCE

FOCUS

especially in this section on Waiting, many tips on how to avoid waiting in line.

 More time for your priorities; less stress.

129. Principles for avoiding

Eleven principles to avoid waiting:

- Arrive on time.
- Come back another time.
- Do it by mail.
- Do it from home.
- Don't do things when others do them.
- Find out what the best hours are.
- Have it delivered, never fetch it.
- Have someone else do it for you.
- Patronize a different vendor.
- Use the phone, catalog or Internet, never your legs.
- Wear your time-urgency.

"DOST THOU LOVE LIFE? THEN DO NOT SQUANDER TIME;
FOR THAT'S THE STUFF LIFE IS MADE OF."
(BENJAMIN FRANKLIN)

130. Punctuality

If people are not on time, you can:

- Attend to other matters while waiting.
- Cancel the appointment.
- Ask them to be more punctual in the future.
- Praise them when they do appear on time: "How wonderful of you to be so punctual. Such a rare quality nowadays!"
- Explain how time-urgent you are.

"HAD WE BUT WORLD ENOUGH, AND TIME, THIS COYNESS,
LADY, WERE NO CRIME."
(ANDREW MARVELL)

131. Reducing waiting

Waiting is usually a terrible waste of time, but you needn't be a king to be spared it. Here are some ways to keep the wait short. (Consult the relevant sections of this book to find more tips.)

- Airport: Don't arrive more than a half hour in advance for domestic flights; check for flight delays. (Travel-Plane)
- Bank: There's rarely a good reason to go. Use ATMs, mail, Web banking. (Computers-Software; Communication-Telephone)
- Hairdresser: Get first appointment of day or afternoon. (Business-Appointments)
- Bus station: Arrive shortly before departure; check for delays. (Travel-Transportation)
- Business appointment: Get first appointment; take work with you. (Business-Appointments)
- Dentist/Doctor: Get first appointment; be frank about time constraints. (Business-Appointments; Health-Medical)
- Fines: You can pay by mail or a messenger service (listed in the Yellow Pages) will go to City Hall for you.
- Friend, appointment with: Agree on maximum waiting time.
- Garage: Leave the car; don't return without confirming it is ready. (Travel-Car)
- Gas Station: Use only automated and less-frequented gas stations. (Travel-Car)
- Government agencies: Use the mail, phone, fax, email, Internet. (Communication-Techniques)
- Home: Be frank with your family about your time urgency; agree on schedules. (Home-Family)
- Hospital: If you can afford a private physician, avoid hospital clinics. Use the emergency room only for emergencies. (Health-Medical)
- Meeting: Start it on time or ask the chair to start; round up colleagues before the meeting. (Business-Appointments)
- Movie: avoid peak times; order tickets by phone or Internet; buy a head-of-the-line pass. (Social/Entertain-Theater)
- Passports: Order and receive by mail.

 TIME-SAVING TIP   INFLUENCE   FOCUS

- Plane tickets: Order by phone or internet, receive by mail or fax (electronic ticketing).
- Post Office: Make your own local post office. (Communication-Mail)
- Registry of Motor Vehicles: Your car dealer's courier will handle registration.
- Restaurants: Only frequent those that take and honor reservations. (Social/Entertain-Restaurants)
- Retail store: Order by phone, catalog, or on the Internet; go off peak hours; delegate. (Home-Shopping)
- Rush tickets: A student may be happy to keep your place in line for a few bucks.
- Supermarket: Order by phone or on the Internet; go off-peak hours; delegate; shop in quantity. (Food-Shopping)
- Taxi stand: Call taxis or hail them on busy streets; schedule town car at small extra expense.
- Telephone calls: no answer, busy or hold—Use auto redial feature and speakerphone. (Communication-Telephone)
- Traffic: Consider subways and alternate modes of transportation (bicycling, walking), off-peak hours, less-frequented routes. (Travel-Commuting)
- Train station: Confirm delays before arriving; arrive shortly before departure. (Travel)

WHILE YOU'RE THERE

132. Do it now A variant of "while you're there" is while you're at it. Say you open a document and read it. Why not take care of it now: handle it, answer it, file it. Otherwise you will have to place it in a tray, glance at it numerous times, and read it again before responding.

Of course, if you want to ponder your response, you may prefer to put it in the projects tray.

133. Empty hands
Reduce multiple trips.

- Use a tray to carry things with you from kitchen to dining room and back.
- Do not return home from shopping only to go out again to another shop: arrange all your stops in a logical sequence.
- Shop in multi-purpose stores such as supermarkets and department stores, or in specialized stores that have large inventories to avoid multiple trips.

134. Gifts
Make a list of the kinds of gifts you need throughout the year for family, friends and colleagues, and occasions such as births, graduations, weddings and divorces, anniversaries, birthdays and holidays.

Aim to buy such gifts not as the event draws near but when it is an efficient use of your time to do so. For example, take the list with you when you travel; you probably will have some time to spare. Keep some extra gifts on hand in a box or "gift closet" in case the perfect personal gift is needed unexpectedly.

135. Layovers
If you find yourself with a few hours' layover, here are some things you can do to use your time rather than waste it:

- Go to a hairdresser (it may be just as good as at home and will save you that much time when you get back).
- Call clients or friends (cell phones make this more feasible than ever, and long distance calls are not that expensive nowadays: clients are worth it and friends are priceless).
- Go through business literature (take notes or tear off interesting pages from catalogs and brochures).
- Clean up your purse or wallet (when did you do it last?).
- Work on a presentation you are to give.
- Read a book.
- Shop for gifts or greeting cards.
- Work on your laptop.
- Review your schedule.

TIME-SAVING TIP   INFLUENCE   FOCUS

136. Opportunity cost

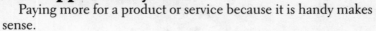

Paying more for a product or service because it is handy makes sense.

> EXAMPLE: While shopping for office supplies you come upon a computer program you have been intending to buy. Maybe you can get it more cheaply from a computer wholesale supplier or catalog. Nevertheless, you should spend more and buy the product now.

Passing up this opportunity comes at a cost: you must check through your catalogs, call the supplier, take the risk they're out of stock, wait for delivery, etc.

Business

APPOINTMENTS

🕐 **137. Avoiding meetings** Sometimes meetings are unavoidable and later we offer several tips to keep them short. To avoid more meetings altogether, however:

- Try delegating responsibilities to individuals who check with the group when necessary by phone or email.
- For brainstorming with others, try a conference call or a website where individuals can post their ideas and reactions for others to see.
- Do not agree lightly to join a group that meets repeatedly: Is this the best way to reallocate your time? Does that group need your specific expertise or just some bodies to comprise a group? Try suggesting another person or sending someone to represent you.

When someone proposes an appointment, consider first if you can solve the issue on the phone, by fax or email. If you are not sure, say: "Let's start this with a phone call and if a meeting proves necessary we'll schedule one." That is, unless you have a special reason for wanting to meet with this person, such as getting to know them better or persuading them of something.

138. Breakfast To avoid spending too much time at business lunches or dinners, have an eight A.M. business breakfast, perhaps in a hotel, before heading to the office by nine.

139. Briefer meetings To speed up your meeting, review this checklist and inform participants beforehand:

- What is the purpose?
- What is the agenda? Assign a time limit to each item.
- Who must attend and what will their roles be? (If there are reliable time-wasters, can you exclude them or encourage them to be brief?)
- Which time and place are the most efficient and likely to be productive? Try to start and end on time. If you often begin late, people will often come late.
- What information must participants have before the meeting?
- What should people be told to bring with them?
- What materials need to be provided?
- Who will record the results and who will disseminate the conclusions? (Consider announcing that the last to arrive will take minutes.)
- Can you anticipate disagreements and resolve them beforehand?

140. Calendar Don't rely on your memory: always check your calendar before accepting an appointment.

141. Calendar If you keep a calendar by hand, consider using colored pencils as well as symbols, arrows and stars to code entries.

142. Calendar You need to have access to a calendar at all times, in the office and outside of it, but it's dangerous to have more than one calendar. Solutions:

- Buy an appointment book that is small enough to be portable.

BENEFITS

BURDENS

BALANCE

- Print out your computerized calendar daily for the next three months and carry those pages with you. Transcribe new appointments and tasks into your desktop computer at the end of the day.
- Buy a palmtop computer that rests in a cradle on your desk and automatically stays synchronized with your desktop.

We like the Hewlett Packard Jornada 430se because it resembles our desktop computer: its operating system (Windows CE) is like the Windows on our desktop, and its Personal Information Manager for contacts, calendar, and tasks (pocket Outlook) is like the Outlook on our desktop computer. (1-800-752-0900)

143. Confirming If asked to reconfirm an appointment at a later date, decline.

- State that the appointment is confirmed and that each person need notify the other only if a change is necessary. Then exchange information on how to notify one another (fax, phone, email . . .) in case there is a change.
- If a restaurant asks you to reconfirm your reservation, say: "I'm sorry, I don't do that, but I'd be happy to give you my charge card number for security." A few may take you up on your offer; most will say it's not necessary.
- Nevertheless, when a business or personal appointment is particularly important to you, consider calling (or sending email) to reconfirm.

144. Consolidate Two separate one-hour appointments require more time than one two-hour appointment—because preliminaries and final remarks take time, as does ushering people in and out of your office. Moreover, two appointments that are not consecutive fragment your day more than consecutive appointments.

Therefore, consolidate. Avoid several short meetings with someone when one longer one will do. Block distinct appointments consecutively.

TIME-SAVING TIP

INFLUENCE

FOCUS

145. Decision makers Sometimes, "Go to the top" is
poor advice because someone junior will be offended and the top
relies on that person's opinion.

More often, though, dealing with anyone other than the decision maker is a waste of time. Worse yet, it may be the junior person you dealt with who presents your case to the decision maker;
normally, you want to do that.

So, find out who is the decision maker and do all possible to
meet with him or her rather than a subordinate. How? See
Strategies-Interpersonal-Getting the decision you want.

146. Ending appointments If you want your
appointment with a visitor to be very short, remain standing. If
you and your visitor are seated, try any of these:

- "It was so nice of you to take the time to come over."
- "I don't want to take more of your time."
- "I better let you go."
- "This is a busy time for both of us, so . . . "
- "It's time for us to stop."

Other graceful ways to end it:

- Summarize the points your discussion has covered.
- Move toward the door, telephone or filing cabinets.
- Have your secretary come in.
- Have someone ring you at the desired time.
- Pre-set an alarm clock or tell your guest at the start how
  much time you have together (don't use round numbers).

147. Lunch Do you really need to "do" lunch? Peter Lynch,
legendary manager of the Magellan Fund, thought eating lunch
out a waste of time; he ate at his desk.

Consider bringing healthy foods with you from home or ordering food to be brought in. You will have time left over to accomplish
things, the more so as the office is quieter during the conventional
lunch hour.

When you do have lunch out, eat earlier or later than the noon
hour and enjoy less crowded restaurants and faster service.

Whether you eat in the office or at a restaurant, do not commit yourself to too many business lunches: They can be produc-

BENEFITS

BURDENS

BALANCE

tive but they take time away from concentrated work such as writing. Select them carefully and limit their duration.

Dining is one of life's pleasures. Besides, sharing a meal with colleagues or friends can bring you closer together.

148. Maps Keep a map near your work area so you can check directions for driving to an appointment and give directions to someone who will be coming to your place of business.

149. Punctuality Be punctual and require that others be so too (within reason). If someone is unacceptably late, tell them if you can that their allotted time has expired. If you agree to rebook the appointment, they will probably be more punctual at your next meeting.

150. Schedule Note in your calendar the time of your outside appointment AND the time at which you should leave the office or your home to arrive on time.

151. Scheduling meetings Rare is the committee that meets once. When you and some colleagues are assembled and decide to meet again, set the date then and there. It is much faster to negotiate the date and time when all participants are present.

Repeated meetings are better attended when they meet in the same place at a regular time and date—such as every Wednesday from three to four; the last Friday of the month, from two to three, etc.

152. Secretary Make friends with the secretary/assistant.

Slip in an honest compliment if you can—you like her voice; you appreciate how helpful she (or he) has been.

Use some humor. If she is hindering you from reaching her boss, tell her how much you would like to have someone like her to screen your appointments. Ask her, confidentially, the best way to get an appointment.

TIME-SAVING TIP   INFLUENCE

FOCUS

153. Setting the scene Leading a meeting or addressing an audience is a performance. Spare yourself time and trouble and check out the scene.

- Is there enough seating and is it arranged as you would like?
- Are you close to your audience (a podium can be a psychological barrier)?
- Is there enough lighting and can you control it readily if there will be slides or other visual presentations?
- If there will be a sign language interpreter, is there a suitable platform and proper lighting?
- Is the space handicap-accessible?
- Is the sound system loud enough? Does it squeal?
- Does the projection equipment work properly with your slides or other materials? Is there a spare bulb?
- Are the slides or transparencies legible from the back of the room?
- Will the room be too warm when filled?
- Will there be distracting noise during your talk, such as waiters clearing tables, a ringing telephone, or sound transmission from an adjacent space or the out-of-doors?

Even if you are satisfied on all these counts, it's a good idea to give the start of your presentation beforehand in the room you will be using, to get the "feel" of the scene; it will put you that much more at ease when the time comes.

154. Stay put As a general rule, it wastes time for you to go anywhere. Try to have your appointments come to you. If that's not feasible, compromise: Propose a site that spares you the full burden of travel time, or propose alternating sites.

Better yet, avoid the meeting in the first place: Is it essential? Could the business be done by email, conference call, videoconferencing, or other means of communication? Can you delegate it? Can the contact be linked to another event that you have decided you must attend? Schedule travel with lead in your shoes; remove it when necessary (or for your pleasure).

A lot of time (and some money) is saved by staying put. Many contacts can be handled cordially in other ways, and your partners to the meeting will appreciate your respect for their time as well.

Personal contact builds relationships and can unearth solutions difficult to find at a distance, so avoiding them may have a cost.

155. Time available In order to avoid spending more time on an appointment than is necessary, you need an estimate of the time required to achieve the goals of that meeting. Ask at the time of booking the appointment, or make an estimate yourself.

> EXAMPLE: "I've set aside a half hour for this meeting; I hope that will prove sufficient." You may feel more comfortable if you are candid about your time consciousness. You are trying to fit a lot into the day these days; you are trying to block time for a major project, etc.

OFFICE

156. Address book Put the names and addresses of people you need to contact in your computer. Computerized Personal Information Managers, such as Microsoft Outlook, will:

- prompt you for all the information,
- drop the address into letters you prepare with your word processor or into email,
- allow you to search by name, city, and such,
- dial the phone number for you if you click on it with your mouse,
- link tasks from your To-Do list to people,
- enter contacts' birthdays as recurring events on your calendar, and
- print out an address book in various formats.

Now, can your Rolodex or pocket address book do all that?

157. Appointments When accepting an outside appointment, take a second to write on your calendar the address and phone number of your host. You won't have to look for them at the last minute.

TIME-SAVING TIP   INFLUENCE   FOCUS

Likewise, when accepting an appointment at your office, exchange phone numbers and provide your address.

158. Banking Normally, there is no reason for you to go to the bank:

- Ask for the name of a banker whom you may call when you have special needs, such as depositing a check in foreign currency, getting a cashier's check by mail, etc.
- Use Checkfree (1-800-882-5280) or other automatic check writing services linked to your money manager software, such as Intuit's Quicken (1-800-446-8848).
- You can get cash and perform many other transactions at your bank's ATM machines.
- Keep track of your accounts and make transfers among them using your bank's website or automated phone service.
- Traveler's checks and foreign currency can be purchased by mail from American Express (1-800-673-3782).

If you absolutely must go to the bank, avoid peak hours: lunch time; the first and last hours of the day; the first and 15th day of the month; days just before holiday weekends.

159. Briefcase A properly equipped briefcase can save you time. Get one with a pocket for miscellaneous items such as an aspirin tin, a comb, a fingernail file, keys etc. There should be a place for pen and pencil and for your calling card. It's nice to have a pocket for diskettes, too. (Staples, 1-800-333-3199)

If you use a beeper, cellular phone, calculator or other device, it is helpful to have pockets for those. An eyeglass pocket is handy, as is a place to carry your contact list with names, addresses and phone numbers.

Since your briefcase will rapidly become an appendage, it is helpful to have a light one. If you carry a lot of documents an expandable case may be right for you.

Many briefcases come with combination locks but in our experience these are more trouble than they're worth—you would never leave your briefcase unattended and, if you did, the entire case can be stolen more quickly than the contents.

BENEFITS

BURDENS

BALANCE

Make a place for your briefcase next to your desk at work and home; empty it at the end of the work day, distributing papers for filing, discard, replacement in the briefcase, etc.

160. Bulletin board If you do not use a computer to keep track of your To-Do list and phone numbers, you may find a bulletin board helpful: you can pin up information you need repeatedly along with reminders, call-back slips, etc. An erasable board will save you a step by allowing you to write directly on the board. Both types are available from Highsmith (1-800-558-2110).

161. Calendar If you want to save time and make progress toward your goals, you must keep a calendar.

- Some people with enviably simple lives use month-at-a-glance calendars that have a box for each of thirty days on one sturdy sheet.
- Then there are more detailed paper-and-pencil calendars combined with contact lists, project sheets and the like, such as Day-Timers (1-800-225-5384) and Franklin Covey (1-800-654-1776).
- These paper calendars have a computerized counterpart, essentially a calendar but with important added features such as varying displays, the ability to search for an entry, easily scheduled recurring events, and printing.
- Computerized Personal Information Managers (like Microsoft Outlook) combine all of these calendar features with to-do lists, scheduling, and an address book. One disadvantage: You must keep updating the printout of your schedule that you carry with you when away from your computer and you must enter new appointments made off-site twice, once on the printout and again on the computer back at home or office.
- Palmtop computers, such as the Hewlett-Packard Jornada 430se (1-800-752-0900) are increasingly popular for people who must schedule events away from their desk (that's most of us). You can drop some palmtops in a holster attached to your computer, which automates schedule updates and spares you double-entry. Moreover, you will always have your task list and address book with you, and you can use

TIME-SAVING TIP

INFLUENCE

FOCUS

other software such as the word processor or spreadsheet (with a little difficulty since the keyboard is small).

162. Clutter

Consider having a small desk and a large wastebasket. Statistics show that the bigger the desk, the greater the clutter. A large basket will be an invitation to discard unnecessary papers.

163. Clutter

Some people with remarkable visual memory can reach into a hodge-podge of mail and papers piled up on their desk and retrieve just the document required.

The rest of us are better advised to use the six trays method (see Business-Office-Sorting) plus a well-organized filing system. We find clutter scary, since tasks can be overlooked up to and past their deadlines. Then, too, searching for a needle in a haystack is no fun.

Understandably, people who rely on you are uneasy if they see a cluttered desk. Can you imagine your surgeon reaching into a haphazard pile of instruments to find the right one?

164. Communicate

Studies show that a major source of wasted time in the business environment is a lack of internal communication. Some steps you can take:

- Use shared folders. If your office is computerized, as most in the U.S. are today, look into setting up a LAN (local area network). That way, all colleagues can use and update the same files (many software programs allow you to keep track of who is changing what in a shared file).
- Send email to a pre-defined list of addressees.
- Send fax.
- Videoconference, teleconference, or meet.
- Notify colleagues off site by regular mail.
- Publish an in-house newsletter or distribute written memoranda.
- Post a progress board where all can see.

165. Corporate credit cards

Get a corporate credit card:

BENEFITS

BURDENS

BALANCE

- Allows convenient payment of creditors here and abroad.
- Safer than employees carrying cash.
- Can be used to get cash from ATM.
- Useful to secure reservations.
- Allows rapid purchasing by phone and by mail.
- Get special rates from car companies, hotels, etc.
- Earn perks such as airline upgrades.

166. Date stamp Whenever you make a note or prepare a longer document, put the date on it. (Word-processing software will do that automatically if you choose).

If you do not date documents, you risk working on an earlier version that has been revised, ending up with two sets of revisions that are difficult to combine.

This way, you can see if things have changed and you also can be sure you are reading the latest updated note rather than an old version which is perhaps obsolete.

167. End-of-day cleanup Take a few minutes at the end of each workday to restore order.

- Clear all the papers off your desk (and out of your briefcase). Discard what can be discarded; set aside for filing those papers that must be filed; place the rest in your in-basket or tickler file (see Home-Office-Tickler file).
- Examine mail, email and voice messages; often you can respond to email on the spot. For voice-mail, make a list on your computer To-Do list or your paper master list of phone calls for the next day (though this may be a good time to call and leave a message and avoid a conversation).
- Mail that requires a response goes into your priority tray (Office-Sorting) or tickler file (Home-Office-Tickler).
- Look at your next day's schedule and at your list of projects. Block off time on your calendar for those you want to work on (make an appointment with yourself). Reschedule the remaining unfinished projects.
- Place documents in your briefcase that you want to process on the way home, at home, or on the way to work (or your first appointment) the next day.
- Now relax, you have done what you could do in the office.

 TIME-SAVING TIP   INFLUENCE   FOCUS

Reduces stress the next day; allows the issues of the next day to germinate in your mind; lowers the risk of overlooking something that needs attention.

168. Filing If you have a good filing system you will find what you need rapidly.

- Appointments. Put them in your calendar; put the paperwork, if any, in your daily or weekly "tickler file." (Instructions for making a tickler file are in Home-Office.)
- Articles. Reference software (like Reference Manager, 1-800-722-1227) allows you to search your database of documents by title, author, topics, comments, and the like, and provides a convenient place to put your comments, as well as a numbering system that can be used for filing the documents. Put the number assigned to each article by the reference database on the first page of the article and file articles in numerical order. Or write the authors' last names and the year of publication on the first page and file the articles in alphabetical order by author and date.
- Books. Use reference software, as with articles. File the books alphabetically by author on your bookshelves. Or sort the books into groups by themes (fiction, nonfiction, reference, etc.) before shelving them alphabetically. This shortens search time and facilitates browsing.
- Letters. If the letter refers to a project for which there is a project folder (see below), the letter is filed there. If it requires a response by a certain date, the letter goes in your tickler file or priority tray. Otherwise, general correspondence can go into an alphabetical file or it can be dropped in back of a chronological correspondence file (best when documents rarely need to be retrieved).
- Memos and Notes. These belong in the tickler file or priority tray if an action is required by a certain date; otherwise they can go in related project files.
- Projects. Make a folder for each project, and group the folders appropriately. For example, a professor might have folders relating to writing projects arranged alphabetically in one file drawer, and those corresponding to projected lecture engagements in chronological order in a second drawer. A travel agent might have one set of folders for clients and another for

airlines. These folders can be records in software, which are easier to search and edit and require no space (see Home Office-Software).

- Publications such as catalogs and magazines. These should be discarded once examined or read unless you find you need to refer to them occasionally. If you do, then they can be stored on library shelves or, more easily, in labeled magazine containers available from any stationery store. Single articles you wish to save can be cut out and filed and their source discarded.
- Reports. Place them on a shelf reserved for documents to be read or in your projects tray. Once read, file them with other reports, books and articles. If they relate to a project file, place a note in that file with the citation and possibly with a copy of your comments (which may also be in the reference data base).

169. Filing Don't let your to-file tray pile up too high. Otherwise, you run the risk of having to search it needlessly every time you can't find a document.

170. Filing—labels For rapid filing and retrieval of documents, file folders with highly readable labels are the answer. You can purchase sheets of blank labels (Avery 1-800-462-8379) and prepare them with your word processor and printer. Make the letters large and bold, so you can spot the file you are looking for more quickly.

171. Flexibility If a change in how you schedule your work would make you happier and more productive, why not consider it or ask your boss to do so?

> EXAMPLE: It takes an hour for you to drive to work because you drive during peak hours. Instead of working 9 to 5, is 10 to 6 feasible?

Thanks to the Internet, a growing number of employees "telecommute"—that is, they often work from home. This can lead to large gains in productivity: commuting time is now available for work, as are short time blocks—for example, after dinner. There may be fewer distractions in the home office, too.

TIME-SAVING TIP   INFLUENCE   FOCUS

Computerized telecommuters can keep their home and office computers in synch with software for the purpose (e.g., LapLink 1-800-343-8080), or simply by carrying modified files between the computers on floppy diskettes or, better because of their larger capacity, Iomega diskettes (requires Iomega drive: 1-800-697-8833). A laptop computer is readily transported between locations (see Computers-Hardware-Laptops); for greatest efficiency it should be equipped with a modem that allows remote access to the Internet and the Local Area Network at the office if there is one.

172. Interruptions Arrange your desk so you are not facing an entrance or corridor. If people cannot catch your eye, they are less likely to interrupt you.

173. Interruptions If you have someone who screens your calls and visitors, you can reduce interruptions by telling them the people who may interrupt you:

- no matter what (boss, spouse, . . .).
- depending on your activity (making telephone calls . . .).
- never (always take a message).

174. Interruptions Leave your office door open and you will often be disturbed. Leave it closed, and you will occasionally miss timely information. A compromise is to keep it half open. Your colleagues will understand that they can disturb you if necessary. An alternative for some settings; hang a Do Not Disturb sign on the door when you wish to work undisturbed.

If the interruptions come from just a few people, sit down with each to examine how the interruptions can be reduced. Consider options such as email; regular "open door" times when you are accessible; voice-mail; allocating some issues to coworkers; brief weekly staff meetings at regular times to exchange information.

If your office is in a cubicle without a door, consider orienting the access toward the aisle that is used least often. If there is room for one, a folding screen will shield you from view.

BENEFITS

BURDENS

BALANCE

175. Meeting reports Notes taken during a meeting are more readily and accurately fleshed out the sooner you sit down to do it. If you drive after the meeting, a memo recorder is handy for this purpose.

176. Meetings

If you decide to attend a meeting:

- Be prepared with your contribution.
- Arrive punctually.
- Do you need to attend the entire meeting? If not, identify the point in the schedule when you can safely leave. You may need to ask the organizer in advance to arrange the agenda so you can leave early.
- Sit near the door, so you can slip out without creating a disturbance, or wait for the break to leave.

177. Meetings Limit the number of attendees at a meeting to those really concerned by that meeting. In that way, you disturb fewer colleagues' work; you increase the chances that the meeting will run smoothly in a short time; and you leave time for those who really need it because they are directly concerned.

178. Meetings

Make sure your meetings are well prepared and well conducted.

- Make an outline of what you want to cover.
- Distribute the outline beforehand.
- Confirm that all concerned will attend.
- Do outside the meeting what need not be done in a group.

179. Meetings Start a meeting early and you may miss some participants.

Start it late and you inadvertently encourage late-comers to arrive at your meetings late.

End the meeting early, no harm. End it late and you will disturb everyone's schedule.

TIME-SAVING TIP

INFLUENCE

FOCUS

180. Meetings The Masonic system for conducting a meeting encourages participation by limiting the length of remarks and maintaining order. First, a chairman is designated. Then each person who asks to speak is allowed to do so without interruption for, say, up to five minutes. No one may ask to speak more than three times.

181. Memo book Books of tear-out memo slips that write through onto a permanent copy page are useful since you will have a record of your messages in chronological order. (Business Book 1-800-558-0220). We prefer the types that list numerous possible messages alongside boxes to check.

182. Part-time To take greater control of your time, consider working part-time instead of full-time, if you can afford it, or divide your working time between company office and home office.

183. Pens Keep a few good pens and pencils handy and chuck the rest. Don't buy ballpoint pens with caps, which are sure to lose their caps and dry out when they do; instead buy retractable ball-points.

184. Photocopying When photocopying without a collator, start with the last page of the document or article and proceed toward the first. In that way the stack of copies will end up in the right order.

185. Post-it notes Post-it notes are great for getting attention, unless your desk is covered by them. Use Post-its only for specific reminders and always stick them in the same place on your desk—e.g., the side of your computer keyboard or monitor.

They can also be used to attach a brief note in a hurry to an outgoing document.

BENEFITS

BURDENS

BALANCE

186. Shorthand If you don't happen to know one of the recognized short hand systems like Pitman, invent one of your own that will save you time when you take notes.

> EXAMPLE: *fu* for follow-up, *tel* for telephone, *dapo* for do all possible, *fyi* for your information, *bec* for because, etc..

187. Sorting Incoming mail falls naturally into six piles; thus we recommend six letter trays within easy reach of your desk. (They can be stacked two or three high.) Related documents in a tray should be clipped or stapled together.

1. Incoming mail just arrived: needs to be opened and sorted.
2. Priority: work on this now. (Example: answer a letter)
3. Longer term projects: (Example: prepare a report)
4. Money matters: (Example: bills to pay; receipts to enter)
5. Completed: to file.
6. Outgoing mail or other documents.

If you prefer folders to trays, consider buying them in a half-dozen different colors and using a color code; yellow = incoming, red = priority, etc.

188. Supplies

FOCUS ON OFFICE SUPPLIES:

To keep your office at home or at work operating efficiently, a variety of office supplies is helpful. Here is our basic list. You can purchase these from any office supply store, by catalog or on the Web. (Highsmith, 1-800-558-2110)

Address book
Business cards
Calculator
Calendar
Clipboard
Computer
Computer diskettes
Envelopes of various sizes

TIME-SAVING TIP

INFLUENCE

FOCUS

Erasers
Filing folders & labels
Filing cabinet
Glue stick
Index cards
Labels
Lead refills
Letter opener
Letter trays
Loose-leaf binders
Loose-leaf supplies
Mailers
Pads
Paper clips
Pencil sharpener
Pens
Phone message pad
Post-its
Postage meter or stamps
Postage scale
Printer
Printer supplies (paper, toner)
Punch, 3-hole
Refills, pens
Rubber bands
Rulers
Scissors
Stapler
Staples
Tape dispenser

BENEFITS

BURDENS

BALANCE

Communications

FAX

189. Answering Many people and businesses send a fax when a letter would suffice in order to make their message appear more urgent.

Just as you discard junk mail unopened and other mail after skimming it, discard faxes readily and respond only to those that require your response.

190. Cover sheet Design a fax cover sheet for use whenever you send a fax. It will provide recipients with:

- your name and address.
- your fax number.
- a number to call if there are problems with fax transmission.
- the number of pages in the fax, so they can be sure they received it all.
- the urgency of your fax.
- a request that the fax be delivered to the addressee promptly.
- the name, title, and phone number of the person to whom the fax is addressed.

191. Deferred sending
Most fax machines or software allow you to send your faxes after a delay, so you can take advantage of the lower telephone rates at certain days and times.

192. Documents
If someone wants to read a document to you on the phone, suggest that they fax it instead.

If the document is in their computer, they could also send it as an attachment to email.

193. Multiple addresses
Use fax to send a document to several addressees.

194. Paper
If you don't want to handle your faxes by computer, buy a fax machine (or fax-printer-scanner combination) that uses plain paper. Machines that use thermal sensitive paper are less expensive but their faxes are difficult to read, to file, and to retransmit.

195. Software
There are many reasons to prefer communications software to a separate fax machine.

- If you own a computer, a modem and a printer, you can send faxes, so you may not need to purchase a fax machine nor find space for it.
- Faxes received by computer can be converted to computer text files more readily for editing.
- It is easier to schedule outgoing faxes to individuals and groups and you need not be present when they are sent.
- You can retrieve your faxes from a remote location.
- A fax machine may jam or run out of paper and shut down. A computer will not.
- You can transmit files of numerical data by fax if your correspondent has the same or compatible software.

You cannot transmit hard copy that you did not prepare on your computer unless you scan it first. If you are liable to receive faxes at any hour, you must always leave your computer turned on.

 BENEFITS BURDENS BALANCE

196. Speeding receipt To be doubly sure of prompt fax receipt, leave a message on your correspondent's voice-mail or answering machine, stating that you have sent them a fax and giving the day and time. State a target time for their response. For example, "It would be especially helpful if I could have your response before noon tomorrow."

MAIL

197. Be brief

"I HAVE MADE THIS LETTER LONGER THAN USUAL, BECAUSE I LACK THE TIME TO MAKE IT SHORT."
(BLAISE PASCAL)

It is an art to say what you have to say briefly and clearly. If you develop that skill, you will save time writing letters, reports, and memos and you will earn the gratitude of your correspondents. To practice conciseness, after writing your next letter or memo, try cutting it by a third.

Condense reports, analysis or minutes of meetings to the essential. Try to cut back on adjectives and adverbs, to use active rather than passive verbs, and to avoid circumlocutions and redundancies.

If you worry that you have been too concise, append the additional material to the letter or report as a clearly marked appendix.

198. Good letters Good business correspondence is like a telephone conversation between colleagues: friendly, explicit, and brief. The best writing reads as if someone were talking to you—in grammatical sentences.

- Make a list of the points you want to cover and put them in a logical order; if the issues are complex, make an outline. Start by giving the background. Then, we recommend this 3-part formula, attributed to P.T. Barnum: "Tell 'em what you're gonna tell them; tell them; tell 'em what you told them."

TIME-SAVING TIP

INFLUENCE

FOCUS

To illustrate: "I am writing to review plans for . . . The choice of site . . . Turning to provisions . . . To keep us on schedule, would you please tell me by . . . whether you approve of these plans for the site and provisions. "

- With each new thought, start a new paragraph, and let the first sentence of that paragraph bridge what has gone before and the new topic.
- Reread and edit your letter—with a word processor, it's easy. Ask yourself whether each sentence is grammatical, yet sounds conversational. Run your spell checker, but inspect the letter for spelling errors (the checker will miss errors that are English words or misspelled proper names).
- Make the letter easy and pleasant to read visually, with enough white space in the borders and between the lines. When possible, it's best to keep the letter to one page. If that's not possible, consider starting the letter with an executive summary that will make the reader want to hear the detailed story. Number the pages.
- Finally, if time permits, put the letter aside for a day or more; when you return to it you will certainly see ways to word parts of it better.

If your letter is clear and explicit your aim in writing is more likely to be achieved. Plus, there will be less need for follow-up contacts.

It is hard to write simply; it feels stressful and it takes time.

199. Handle once How many times do you handle each piece of mail? The time-wise goal for much mail is "only once." To see how you're doing, place a check mark or write the date at the top of each piece of mail each time you pick it up.

If you find you have many letters with multiple check marks, consider these options for each:

- Throw the damn thing out; if you haven't responded by now, it probably isn't a priority.
- Respond now or take whatever action is required and be done with it.
- Ask someone else to respond (your spouse, your assistant . . .).

- Enter the issues you want to address on your To-Do list or in your calendar, then file the letter.
- At least make notes on the letter each time you review it, so the task of answering will grow easier.

200. Labels

The easy way to do repeated mailings to the same addressees is to use word processing software to duplicate text and to address envelopes or mailing labels.

You can also prepare a set of mailing labels by hand or typewriter and have it photocopied onto sheets of adhesive labels.

EXAMPLE: You send your quarterly tax bills to the ABC mortgage company. Using the Labels feature of your software, you prepare some sheets of adhesive labels with ABC's address and file them in the mortgage folder.

EXAMPLE: Using your contacts manager, you print the envelopes for your holiday cards in a handsome cursive script with just a few clicks of the mouse.

201. Marginal notes

An efficient way to respond to mail is to write on the original and mail or fax it back to the source.

(If you have a secretary, he or she can use the notes to prepare a more formal reply.)

202. Objectives

If you are writing to someone because you want them to do something, the best strategy requires you to:

- Be clear in your own mind about your behavioral objectives. Do you want them to provide you with certain information? Carry out a request? Specifically, what do you want them to do?
- How is it in their interest to do that? Is this a step toward a shared goal?
- State your objectives clearly in your letter. You may want to number the points.
- Summarize those objectives in the closing lines of the letter.

TIME-SAVING TIP

INFLUENCE

FOCUS

203. Photocopying Consider buying a personal or small business photocopier for your home. You will use it more than you expect.

- You want to file a document for easy retrieval but there are two or more folders that are appropriate. Photocopy it and place a copy in each.
- You choose to write your response to a letter on the original, but want to retain a copy for your records.
- You want to send proof of purchase but need to keep the original.

Machines that print, scan, and photocopy are on the market (e.g., Brother MFC 8600 1-800-276-7746). Before you buy, consider: If you have a scanner and separate printer you can use your computer to reproduce documents. Fax machines will also do sheet photocopying.

204. Post cards Consider using post cards rather than letters.

- Saves money on materials and postage.
- Saves time (no folding, inserting, and sealing).
- Smaller size invites short hence rapid answer.
- You can purchase postal reply cards or insert a postcard in a letter to hasten the reply. It takes your correspondent only a moment to confirm receipt of your materials or to check off some alternatives you have listed on the reply card.

205. Postman Did you know that the postman will pick up outgoing mail from your box when he or she leaves the incoming mail? This will save you trips to the letterbox.

206. Stamps
You can save time by rarely going to the post office.

- Buy stamps by phone (1-800-247-8777).
- Your postman will give you an order form and deliver the stamps to you.

BENEFITS

BURDENS

BALANCE

- Rent a postal meter for as little as $20 per month (Pitney Bowes, 1-800-835-4204).
- Use the Internet to put postage on your letters. Stamps.com integrates well with MS Word and Outlook and with Word Perfect so you can print the postage bar code on the envelope you are addressing without leaving the word processor. However, there are several drawbacks compared to using a postage meter. You must be constantly connected to the Internet; you may have to modify addresses in your files, because a specific format is required; you may not frank mail addressed overseas nor pre-printed envelopes; special labels are required for franking window envelopes. If you do not have a line to the Internet, you may sign up with Estamp.com, which uses a device attached to your PC.
- You will need a scale, available from any office supply store (e.g., Staples: 1-800-333-3199) and a chart of domestic and international postal rates, available by calling the rates desk of your main post office or by printing information from the Web at: www.usps.com.
- You can order stamp delivery by mail at the postal service website with a credit card (www.usps.com).

207. Thank you notes There are times when you want to send a word of thanks but your good intentions get crowded out.

If you buy thank you cards (or make some of your own with your word processor), it takes but a moment to add a personal word or two, address the envelope, and frank it. This will probably take less time than calling the person but more time than email.

The time you apparently put into your expression of thanks is a sign of your appreciation. Printed messages, envelopes and postage undercut your message.

208. Travel correspondence If you print address labels from your computerized address book or write them out before you leave on a trip, you will be able to send cards and letters en route more easily.

TIME-SAVING TIP   INFLUENCE   FOCUS

209. Unwanted mail To remove your name from many ①
national mailing lists, write to: Direct Marketing Association,
Mail Preference Service, Box 9008, Farmingdale, NY, 11735

TECHNIQUES

210. Comparison

Before you communicate, take a moment to consider your ①
options:

- Phone: cheap, fast but your party may be out or engage you
  in conversation, no way to trace.
- Mail: slow and costly to create, delayed arrival.
- Fax: cheap, fast, leaves trace. Addressee need not be present.
  Print quality degraded.
- Email: Cheap, fast, leaves trace, highly legible.

211. Handwriting When you have to send a fast letter, ①
note or memo, consider handwriting: It can be faster than using
a typewriter or computer and printer.

⚖ Furthermore, handwriting has a special charm and adds a personalized touch.

212. Memo recorders Memo recorders are a handy ①
way to "jot down" notes without paper and pencil and visual
attention. Hence they are especially convenient in an automobile. (American Voyager, 1-800-515-5110)

Some now come with voice recognition software to turn your
patter into text. (L & H Voice Express Mobile Professional 1-800-
537-6688)

👍 Important thoughts will not get lost; you can use "dead time" to
make plans, record ideas etc.

Devices with a reasonable storage capacity can cost around $100. You have to play back the recording at a later time which is slower than scanning notes.

213. Voice-mail If a secretary offers to take your phone message, ask instead for voice-mail.

- It takes much longer to leave your message with a human being, and the manner of delivery is out of your hands.
- Leave a detailed message, sparing your correspondent the need to track you down for essential information. Include the day and time and the best way for the person to contact you.
- If there are many details, you may prefer to send a fax.

214. Answering When you answer the phone (or when others or a device answer for you) anticipate the information that the caller probably needs.

Callers generally do not need to know the number they just dialed. They frequently need to know, or have confirmed, the person they reached and the office, if it is a business call. If you answer the phone by saying your name (and your office if need be), this will spare both parties the pointless duet: "May I speak with Mr. X please?" "This is Mr. X."

215. Answering machine If you want to leave someone a message but not engage in a conversation:

- Call when they are likely to be out and their answering machine responds.
- Call their voice-mail number.
- Send them email.
- Send them a fax.

 TIME-SAVING TIP   INFLUENCE   FOCUS

TELEPHONE

216. Answering machine If you're away from home and want to remember something important when you get home, call your answering machine. It will remind you when you listen to your messages upon your return.

217. Ask their name It is good practice to note the name of the person with whom you are dealing on the telephone.

Ask their name after volunteering your own. The mere fact that you asked their name may bring you better service.

At the end of the conversation, ask for their direct dial number and the best days and times to reach them; note those, too, in your contacts list or address book.

"You have been so competent and friendly, I'd like to be able to reach you again if necessary."

The next time you call, you will have the name of someone to ask for, someone who has background on your issue.

218. Automatic redial Many local phone companies now offer an automatic redial that will repeatedly try the busy number you dialed until you get through. Try dialing *66 next time you get a busy signal.

You may need to subscribe for this service and pay a fee.

219. Best times to call Make a note of the best times to reach people. You can ask them for that information or be guided by their profession.

Business people usually have meetings on Monday mornings, TV people stay late at night, publishers take long lunches, etc. Tradesmen commonly leave their office shortly after it opens (quite early). Give white collar workers 30 minutes after opening, enough time for late arrivals, greetings, and the first cup of coffee. Call:

ACCOUNTANTS: between April 21 and Christmas
BANKERS: 9–10 A.M., 3–4:30 P.M.

BENEFITS

BURDENS

BALANCE

DENTISTS: 8:30–9:30 A.M.
DOCTORS: 8:30–9:30 A.M., 4:30–5 P.M.
EXECUTIVES: 10:30–11:30 A.M., 2–5 P.M.
HOMEMAKERS: mid-morning, mid-afternoon
LAWYERS: 11 A.M.–12 P.M.; 4–5 P.M.
LITERARY AGENTS: 10:30–11:30 A.M., 3:30–4:30 P.M.
RETAIL BUSINESSES: 1–3 P.M.
STOCKBROKERS: 9–10 A.M., 3–5 P.M.
TEACHERS: 4–5 P.M.

220. Brief calls Want to keep a call brief? Tell the other person.

Example: " I only have a minute but I did want to get back to you . . . "

221. Calling back Occasionally there are urgent calls that must be returned as quickly as possible, even at the cost of interrupting a block of time devoted to some project.

Most often, however, call-back can wait and fill the little gaps in the day's schedule that are about the right size—as when you have a few moments waiting for a visitor to arrive or a meeting to begin.

Another good time for call-back is at the end of the day, when you are less inclined to start work on a new project.

222. Calls to make To keep track of the people you need to call, the topic, and the dates on which you left messages:

- Make an entry for each on your To-Do list or calendar; or
- Note each on an index card.
- Arrange the calls in order of importance. If you cannot reach someone on the list, don't dwell on it, proceed to the next person.
- You are not obliged to call every person who called you. You can send them email, or you can do nothing at all.

223. Cellular phone If you buy a cellular phone and a hands-free holster for your car, you will be able to make and receive calls no matter where you are. Some cellular phones allow you to use your laptop for email, faxing and Internet browsing.

 TIME-SAVING TIP   INFLUENCE   FOCUS

Others have built-in email and a mini-browser for the Internet.

The cell phone is particularly valuable if you spend time away from your desk; you can handle business and personal calls at the same time that you are walking on an errand or driving to some destination.

Get a spare rechargeable battery. If your phone battery goes dead, you will have another one ready to work, without waiting a few hours to recharge the dead one. If your car breaks down or you can't find your host's address, you will be glad you have a phone in your car.

Almost all cell phones store numbers—usually 100 at a minimum, and allow you to assign names and identities to those numbers. Some offer voice-dialing (and voice memos).

224. Conference calls When conferring with more than one friend or colleague is needed, don't think meeting, think conference call.

Agree with each party on a time for your telemeeting. A few minutes before, enter the code numbers required (ask your phone company or long-distance carrier) and the two or more phone numbers—and voila.

225. Cord Get a long cord for your telephone headset: You can go on doing other things while speaking on the phone instead of being confined to your desk or telephone table at home. Roll-up devices for long cords are available.

Better yet, buy a cordless phone. You can even get a hands-free version that includes a very lightweight headset—then you are truly free to work around the house or office while using the telephone. Department and appliance stores sell these phones, as does Radio Shack (1-800-843-7422).

Wireless telemarketer's-type headsets are available with a base station that connects to a standard phone jack. You will be able to move about and do other things while you're speaking on the phone. You may spare yourself some neck cramps or injury.

226. Don't answer Is the phone driving you crazy? Does it ring every time you settled down to work on a complex task? Are you ready to scream? We thought so.

BENEFITS

BURDENS

BALANCE

Shut the damn thing off. Forget screening messages—that's distracting, too. Shut off the ringer, and let your secretary, (silent) answering machine or voice-mail receive the call.

Then, review your messages when you have a break and schedule the call-backs. If you have an email address, encourage your callers to use it; when asked for your phone number, suggest email; when leaving a message, leave your email address rather than your phone number.

 227. Eavesdropping Filtering calls is distracting, but not as distracting as answering them all. Set your answering machine or voice-mail software to eavesdropping, so you can filter calls and answer only when it suits you.

Another way to filter calls is to sign up for the telephone company service "caller ID" that displays the phone number of the person or business calling you.

You are particularly vulnerable to nuisance calls at home between 6 and 8 P.M. because solicitors know that's the best time to find you in. You may decide not to answer the phone during those hours or to filter the calls.

 228. Getting through Here are some options if you find you are calling someone repeatedly without reaching them.

- Ask their secretary to make a telephone appointment and enter it in their calendar.
- Ask if your party minds receiving calls at home.
- Try to get their direct number (ask them for it, or ask the switchboard or secretary, or consult a published phone list).
- Call a little before the start of the workday or a little after, or during lunch.
- Call a mutual contact and ask their advice on how to get through to your party.
- Call the person's supervisor and explain your problem.
- Send them a fax or email. It can be substantive, or simply say that you will be calling on certain days and times.
- Send the message to them by courier.
- Sit outside their door (but take work with you, as you may be there for a while).

 TIME-SAVING TIP   INFLUENCE   FOCUS

- Do not accept promises of a call-back in the first place. Say, instead, that it may be difficult to reach you, and so you will call back—and then ask for the best time and date to do so.
- For people you are likely to be calling, note the time at which they call you. That may be a good time to catch them in and available.

If there is a secretary controlling which calls get prompt attention, you need that person's help. Find out their name and use it; be cordial on the phone (smiling while you speak may help) and recognize that they are trying to do their best at an important job.

If you meet, acknowledge that you have spoken on the phone and express appreciation for their help. Encourage friendly contacts between that secretary and your own, if you have one.

Learn something about the secretary, such as where he or she is from and bring that up when and if it is appropriate. In short, view the secretary as a junior partner in your collaboration.

229. Hang up
When it is time to end a call:

- Say so: " Let me summarize, as I have to end now . . . "
- Hang up immediately after your closing remarks: "I'll get back to you then." Click.

230. Home
Save steps and place telephone extensions where you need them often—kitchen, bathroom, hallway, perhaps your bedroom. For little extra expense, you can buy telephones that will serve as intercoms and also receive voice-mail.

231. Location
If you're right handed, place your telephone on your left so your right hand will be free to take notes.

232. Menus
Telephone menus save the company money by wasting your time.

Not only do you have to listen to sets of choices that don't interest you, but frequently you arrive at the end without hearing the option you require.

BENEFITS

BURDENS

BALANCE

Remember the days when there were no menus and the representative listened to your reason for calling, then referred you appropriately?

In many cases you can go back to the good old ways by not playing their game. When asked to "press 1 if you have a touch-tone phone," do nothing or press 0. Often, an operator will respond and refer you appropriately.

If you find that you are forced to use a menu, make a note of the numeric choices next to the telephone number; that will speed your call—until the day they change the menu.

 233. Message content Messages you leave on voice-mail or an answering machine should contain at least the following information, in this order:

1. Identify yourself.
2. State the purpose of your call.
3. Say explicitly what you would like your correspondent to do.
4. Give a target date or time for its completion or for some milestone.
5. If you have asked them to contact you by phone or it appears that they may need to, tell them the best times to call and the number to call. (Say the numbers slowly and clearly.)
6. Give them your email address.
7. Identify or allude to the payoff for your correspondent taking the desired action. Often, this will be progress toward a larger goal.
8. Express your thanks.

 234. On hold Don't you hate to be put on hold? It's so rude!

Many companies make money at your expense by under-staffing their phone lines and putting you on hold. Airlines, tech support and major restaurants are particularly bad offenders. Don't believe them when they say "Your call is important to us." If it were, you wouldn't be on hold. Here are some things you can do to stop them from wasting your time on hold:

• Hang up. If enough people hung up, they would provide better service.
• Take your business elsewhere.

TIME-SAVING TIP

INFLUENCE

FOCUS

- Shop on the Web.
- Start the conversation, with "Please don't put me on hold." If it happens anyway, hang up and call back later, if you must call back.
- Purchase a speakerphone that allows you to put them on hold when they put you on hold. You can work knowing that you will hear your correspondent come back on line.
- When you are connected with your party, ask them what days and times are their peak hours and avoid those in the future. (Of course, they reduce staffing in off-peak hours so this may not help.)

235. Ordering When dealing with a merchant by phone, their representative will sometimes ask you to wait while they perform some operation, such as obtaining credit card approval. Ask to be excused while they complete the transaction.

236. Pagers Pagers are smaller, lighter, and cheaper than many cell phones. Numeric pagers tell you the calling number. Alphanumeric pagers allow you to read some text as well. A PCMCIA pager connects to your laptop, so you can see an extended message on your screen. Some pager companies allow you to send text from your computer. Wristwatch pagers are increasingly available.

Pagers work nationwide, have great battery life, and work inside buildings. If someone urgently needs to reach you, they can. But you control when the telephone conversation will take place.

237. Pen and pad You should have pad and pencil next to each telephone extension. Since pencils and pens tend to wander off, buy the kind that comes attached to a self-adhesive holder.

238. Phone book When you look for a number in the phone book, circle or highlight that number so it will be easier to spot next time you look for it. Of course, if you intend to use it often, put it down in your Rolodex, address book or computer.

BENEFITS

BURDENS

BALANCE

239. Preparation Take just a minute to make a list of topics you want to cover (in decreasing order of importance) as you go to make your next phone call.

Write the list of topics next to the name when you enter it in your To-Do list; or write it on the letter or other document that led to the call.

Assemble the relevant files or papers before you make the call. If the purpose of the call is to make an appointment, choose a few times in advance that suit your schedule.

You will save time, too, if you take notes during or just after your conversation. Write them into a file or in the notes section of your contacts manager.

240. Solicitation Never respond to telephone solicitation, just say, " I never respond to telephone solicitation."

Even one weak moment can be your downfall because soliciting companies regularly share lists of potential clients.

If the caller is conducting a survey, decline to participate and hang up—unless for some reason you want to spend time answering their questionnaire.

If the caller represents a charity, tell them you do all your giving in one focused area. Choose that one area carefully: Is it a reputable charity? What percent of their charitable revenues are spent on administration? Pledge and contribute by mail not by phone. Do not provide your phone number.

241. Speed dialing Many telephones feature speed dialing: You place the number you want to call in the telephone memory and link it to a speed dial button on the telephone.

Software to manage contacts, such as MS Outlook, allows you to dial automatically after clicking on the contact and on auto dial.

242. Unlisted number If you don't want to be disturbed by too many phone calls but wish nonetheless to be available to a few select people who may call, ask the telephone company for an unlisted number and give that out to the few.

TIME-SAVING TIP

INFLUENCE

FOCUS

243. Voice-mail Of course you have an answering machine, but have you considered the advantages of computerized voice-mail at work and at home?

1. At work, voice-mail invites the caller to leave a message OR to press a certain number to get an assistant, operator etc., so the caller need never go without speaking to someone.
2. At work or home, it's a snap to change the message depending on your schedule and activities that day.
3. If some people will be calling for predictable information, such as driving instructions, they can reach the "mailbox" with that recorded information by pressing a given number.
4. In your message, reassure the caller that you call in for messages throughout the day.
5. Tell the caller what key to press to bypass the message and start recording.
6. At home, separate mailboxes can be used for each member of the family, thus sparing each the time wasted listening to messages not addressed to them.
7. Keep your message brief.
8. Call your number and listen to your message. Is this how you want to present yourself to people who do not know you?

Win Fax has a companion voice-mail system for your computer called Talkworks (1-800-441-7234).

Computerized voice-mail requires a computer, typically left on all the time, and some software whose use must be mastered.

TELEPHONE LISTS

244. Mini-lists Print out or photocopy your contacts list in reduced size. Keep copies in your home, office, glove compartment. You may even want to carry a list of most frequent contacts and their numbers in your wallet or purse.

BENEFITS

BURDENS

BALANCE

245. Pencil If you keep a contact list by hand and not by computer, we suggest you use pencil as people's addresses and phone numbers change.

246. Professions Some contacts, especially frequent ones, are best remembered by name. Others, such as tradesmen, are more readily retrieved by trade or profession. If you use software to manage your contacts, there is likely a profession field that you can fill in and later use for searches. If you use an address book, simply enter the profession alphabetically (as you would a last name).

247. Rolodex You may not want to leave your address book lying about and there is likely no computer terminal near the family phone, so a Rolodex next to that phone, with phone numbers of friends, restaurants, airlines, etc., can be quite useful.

You may prefer to have a single list, however, that you can print out or photocopy for multiple locations.

TIME-SAVING TIP

INFLUENCE

FOCUS

Computers and the Internet

HARDWARE

248. Advantages Focus on Things a Computer Can Do for You (And the software that does it, with our recommended choice of software.)

- ADDRESS BOOK: Maintain an address book (Microsoft Outlook).
- APPOINTMENTS: Schedule appointments, take linked notes (Microsoft Outlook).
- CORRESPONDENCE: Send email over the Internet (email programs: Microsoft Outlook).
- CALENDAR: Maintain and print your calendar and make searches easy (Microsoft Outlook).
- TASKS: Maintain a To-Do list (Microsoft Outlook).
- PHONE CALLS: Schedule, dial, and record phone calls (Microsoft Outlook).
- WORD PROCESSOR—Documents: Prepare letters, reports, and other documents (Microsoft Word).
- MAILING: Print labels and envelopes (Microsoft Word).
- SPREADSHEETS—Calculations: Perform complex financial calculations (Microsoft Excel).
- GRAPHICS: Design advertising, charts, slide shows, and other displays (Microsoft PowerPoint).
- PRESENTATIONS: Create presentations with text, graphics, and sound (Microsoft PowerPoint).

- CHECKBOOK: Maintain and balance your checkbook (money manager: Intuit Quicken).
- FAX: Convert fax to a text file for editing (communications software: Symantec Winfax).
- FAX: Send and receive faxes (communications software: Symantec Winfax).
- FINANCE: Prepare expense reports (money manager: Intuit Quicken Expensables).
- GAMES: Entertain you and you and your friends with games (we don't recommend this software if you are trying to save time).
- HEALTH: Track nutritional intake (Analyzer for Windows), Track group or family nutrition or diet plans (FitBody Pro), Track workouts, measurements, weight and goals (ProTrack 99 Fitness software) (see Health & Recreation-Sports-Fitness software).
- INTERNET: Connect to computer information services and the Internet, allowing you to send and receive files, electronic mail, and information on news, weather, and sports; business and finance; electronic shopping; research and reference; travel and leisure. See also Internet-Connection. (Internet browser: Microsoft Explorer).
- PAPER CONVERSION: Scan documents into a file for insertion in other documents or for conversion to text (communications software, and Optical Character Recognition software: Omnipage Pro), or simply for convenient storage and retrieval. Equipment options: handheld, flatbed or all-in-one scanners.
- PROJECTS: Manage tasks, allocate time to various tasks (project manager: Microsoft Project).
- RECORDS: Maintain a data base, for example, employee records (database software: Microsoft Access).
- STOCKS: Maintain your portfolio (money manager: Intuit Quicken).
- TAX: Maintain tax records (money manager: Intuit Quicken).
- TAX: Prepare your tax return (tax preparation software: QuickenTaxCut).

The Microsoft products are best purchased as an integrated package, Microsoft Office: 1-800-426-9400. The programs are

TIME-SAVING TIP

INFLUENCE

FOCUS

designed to work well together. The package is expensive but upgrades are not.

Symantec: 1-800-441-7234

Intuit: 1-800-446-8848

Caere:1-800-535-7226

 You will create, store and retrieve information more rapidly and more effectively

 It takes time and money to buy the right computer for your needs, and time to familiarize yourself with the hardware and software.

249. Installing your computer

The words "Some Assembly Required" have been known to bring otherwise strong men and women to tears. If you are one of those but want to buy a computer, here's good news.

Some computer manufacturers like IBM (1-800-426-4968) and sales companies like CompUSA (1-800-266-7872) offer to preload the software programs you need. Other companies will set up your equipment for a modest fee. (Check your Yellow Pages under "Computer Dealers" and "Computer System Designers and Consultants.")

Leap at the opportunity! Let experienced people make sure that the components of your system and the various software programs you require will work well together. Computers that are touted as a "snap" to set up rarely are.

250. Laptops

Laptop computers are essential for the businessman or woman on the go, but they are also mighty useful for the rest of us. Some are as thin as a notebook, and weigh under three pounds. At that weight, don't expect a lot of built-in devices such as CD-ROM or a Zip drive (for backup): you will have to buy them as plug-ins.

If you use your laptop extensively, you will prefer a larger portable which allows a bigger keyboard and screen and some of those notebook plug-ins built in. With your laptop you can make

BENEFITS
BURDENS
BALANCE

travel time work for you—take care of correspondence, write reports, take notes on reading, send and receive faxes and email, etc. Software for remote access (such as Symantec's PC Anywhere) will allow you to work with the files on your desktop computer using your laptop.

IBM Thinkpad notebooks 1-800-426-7255

Symantec: 1-800-441-7234

👍 You can turn dead time into productive time in an airplane, a hotel room, or anywhere away from your desktop. Productivity increases, work can be more timely, and the pressure is less when you return to your home base.

👎 These miracles of miniaturization are costly, ranging from two to ten thousand dollars, depending on features. And a full-featured laptop and batteries weigh in at a hefty six or seven pounds.

🕐 **251. Maintenance**
Your computer, like your car, needs regular maintenance.
- Make rescue diskettes using Norton Utilities;
- Schedule automatic backup with Microsoft's Mybackup or Seagate's Backup exec.
- Click Start>Programs>Accessories>system tools> and choose maintenance wizard (Windows 98) or
- run Scandisk or Norton Disk Doctor (to check for hard disk errors)
- run defrag or Norton Speed Disk (to defragment your hard disk).

👍 Avoid catastrophic loss of files (backup); a place to turn when files are deleted, revised or corrupted in error (backup); forestall hard disk errors (scandisk); speed up processing (defrag).

🕐 **252. Palmtops** Palmtops are great for maintaining up-to-date calendars and contact lists in two places—on your main PC and on your person. Be sure to get one with a cradle and automatic synchronization software. Verify that the brand you buy will

 TIME-SAVING TIP   INFLUENCE   FOCUS

synchronize with the desktop software you use. For example, the HP Jornada 430se comes loaded with a pocket version of Windows called Windows CE and MS Outlook 2000 calendar, scheduler, and a version of MS Word for word processing. When you place your palmtop in the cradle attached to your PC, it will update the PC files with any changes you have made to those files on your palmtop, and vice-versa.

Be sure the palmtop you buy has a built-in backup battery in case the rechargeable battery runs down.

Check whether the keyboard is too small for you. Some palmtops come without keyboards—you write on a screen instead. However, it takes some practice to learn to write in a way that allows the computer to recognize your printing correctly.

253. Scanners

- Handheld scanners are compact and easy to use but they generally scan only a portion of a document at a time; the software integrates the separate scans into a page format.
- Flatbed scanners can do entire pages and tend to yield a better quality scan.
- Scanners in all-in-one units (Fax, Printer, Scanner, Copier) only scan sheets of paper, no books, and the scan quality is often substandard.

254. Speed The moral of the story:

When buying a new computer, buy as much memory, speed, and storage capacity as you might possibly need and then some. The story:

The computer industry has been improving on memory, speed and storage at a terrific clip: Whatever computer you buy today will be a dinosaur in three years because the latest software performs best on the latest machines. To get good performance and delay your computer's obsolescence, get in front of the curve.

255. Surge protector Buy a surge protector to avoid damage to your computer if there is a power surge. A SmartUPS uninterruptible power supply (APC Corp. 1-800-800-4272) gives protection from brown out and spikes. If power is lost, the unit

BENEFITS

BURDENS

BALANCE

supplies battery power to the computer. When the battery is depleted, it commands the computer to shut down properly. Sure, it costs more than a ten-dollar power strip with surge protection, but a surge strip only protects you once: If a momentary voltage spike trips the surge strip and you reset it, the strip will not protect against another spike, although it will still supply power to your computer.

When you lose power to your office or home, shut your computer off and unplug it so that the power surge when the service comes back on will not harm it.

256. What to buy Most people today buy IBM personal computers (PCs) or computers that are compatible with IBM, although there are many loyal Macintosh users, especially in fields such as design and computer graphics.

Here are the features to discuss with the salesperson (and our suggestions). CAUTION: Computer technology is evolving rapidly and software evolves to take advantage of the new capabilities.

HARD DRIVE (7 gigabytes; you need a minimum of 5)
MONITOR (17 in, multimedia)
MEMORY (128 megabytes)
SYSTEM (Pentium III processors, 450 MHz or higher clock)
BACKUP DEVICE (tape drive or writable CD ROM driver)
MODEM (voice-fax, 56 K)
PRINTER (Laser)
DRIVES (3 ½-inch diskette, CD-ROM; Iomega drive)
SURGE PROTECTOR

A good computer will make you more accurate, rapid and productive in performing numerous tasks.

Computers that are versatile and rapid are not cheap. Expect to spend about four thousand dollars for the package we have described.

257. Your workstation You will be able to use your computer for longer periods at work or at home without risking injury if the physical arrangement is ergonomically correct.

TIME-SAVING TIP INFLUENCE FOCUS

KEYBOARD: 23 to 28 inches above the floor.

MONITOR BASE: 27 to 32 inches above the floor.

LEGROOM UNDER THE WORKSTATION: 27 x 27 inches minimum.

CHAIR HEIGHT: adjustable, 16 to 20 inches.

SEAT: 18 inches wide, 15–17 inches deep; 4 in clearance between seat front edge and backs of the knees.

SEAT BACK: backward tilt 90 to 105 degrees, should provide gentle pressure against your lumbar area.

BACKREST: 12 inches wide minimum, 6–9 inches of support centered 6–10 inches above the seat.

SEAT PAN ANGLE: fixed between 0 and 10 degrees to support thigh and buttocks.

POSITION THE KEYBOARD MONITOR AND CHAIR SO THAT: Your forearms and hands are parallel to the floor when using the keyboard and adjacent mouse; your thighs are horizontal; feet flat on the floor; head 18 to 28 inches from the monitor, with the top of the screen slightly below eye level.

Do not place the monitor with its back to or directly facing windows. Instead, position the window (if you're lucky enough to have one) on your left, and the monitor directly in front of you, so the light coming from the window will not reflect off the screen nor fall directly in your eyes.

Less danger of injury, less fatigue, higher productivity.

Fully adjustable desks and chairs can be expensive.

INTERNET

258. Advantages The World Wide Web is the vast collection of documents available over the Internet worldwide. There is something for everyone. To find your somethings, you need access to the Internet and an Internet program such as Microsoft's Internet Explorer.

BENEFITS

BURDENS

BALANCE

- You can use the Net to send and receive email. (See Computers-Internet-Email.)
- You can search the Web for any topic, using any of several search engines, which are themselves sites on the Web. (See Computers-Internet-Search Engines.)
- Countless companies are on the internet and you can purchase materials and services at their sites. (See Computers-Internet-Shopping.)
- Like them, you can create your own home page on the Internet, where you can provide information about yourself, your family or your business.

In the following tips, we offer a few of the major Internet addresses under some of the more popular topics: banking, books, careers, computer software and hardware, entertainment, food, government, home, insurance, medicine and health, minorities, personal finance, pets, reference materials, search engines, shipping, shopping, stocks and bonds, and travel.

259. Banking

www.bankone.com
www.bankamerica.com
www.barclays.co.uk
www.chase.com
www.checkfree.com
www.citicorp.com
Federal Reserve Bank of New York: www.ny.frb.org
Fleet Bank: www.fleet.com
www.usbank.com
www.wellsfargo.com

260. Books

You can purchase new and out-of-print books on the Web. Useful addresses:

Advanced Book Exchange: www.abe.com
www.Amazon.com
Barnes & Noble: www.BN.com
www.Bibliofind.com

TIME-SAVING TIP

INFLUENCE

FOCUS

www.Bookfinder.com
www.Bookpricer.com
www.BookSearchEngine.com
Independent booksellers: www.BookSense.com
www.Interloc.com

261. Careers

www.americasemployers.com
America's Job Bank: www.ajb.dni.us
Au Pair Job match Service: www.aupairs.co.uk
www.careerpath.com
www.acareer.com
www.careermart.com
www.careermosaic.com
Fedworld Federal Job Search: www.fedworld.gov/jobs/job-search.html
www.job-hunt.org
www.jobtrak.com
www.kellyservices.com
www.manpower.com
www.freelanceonline.com
www.jobfind.com

262. Computer hardware
You can purchase computers and get technical support on the Web. If you know the manufacturer, go to these sites:

www.apple.com
www.IBM.com
www.Compaq.com
www.dell.com
Gateway: www.gw2k.com
Hewlett Packard: www.HP.com
www.pcmall.com

If you want to window-shop and perhaps buy from a dealer, try these addresses:

www.PCConnection.com
www.Cnet.com
www.Compusa.com

BENEFITS

BURDENS

BALANCE

⏱ 263. Computer software
www.microsoft.com
www.symantec.com
www.lotus.com

264. Connection
You need four things to have access to the wonders of the Internet: software that allows you to use the Internet (called a browser), a computer to run the software, a connection to the Net, and an Internet service provider, such as America On Line.

Some ways to get connected to the Net:

- Buy a 56K modem and plug it into (or install it inside) your computer. A modem is useful for sending and receiving faxes and, with software such as Winfax, can also serve as an answering machine. But it is a poor way to connect to the Net because it is painfully slow in transferring information from the Net onto your computer screen and vice-versa. One-time cost for the device, about $200. Try 3Com 56K Voice faxmodem pro (800-638-3266).

- Subscribe to ISDN service. Your local cable television supplier may provide this service, which, like cable TV, requires leading a wire to your house and to your equipment—in this case, your computer. Monthly cost for the service, about $45.

- Subscribe to ADSL (Asymmetric Digital Subscriber Line). Up to ten times faster than ISDN in downloading information onto your screen but that depends on your distance from the nearest telephone company central office—the limit is 18,000 feet. It is slower in sending information upstream, from your computer to the Net. Check with your telephone company—they may offer DSL using your phone line. If they do not, try InternetConnect (1-800-896-7467). Cost: about $60 a month. You will need to buy a modem and an Ethernet card.

- Symmetrical DSL. The fastest Internet connection generally available and the most costly—about $80 a month. You'll need the modem and Ethernet card here too.

TIME-SAVING TIP

INFLUENCE

FOCUS

265. Cooperative solutions Cooperative businesses exist for countless purposes: Credit unions, banks, insurance, food, housing, health, energy, funeral homes, preschool, child care, and more. You can learn about these and others from the website of the National Cooperative Business Association: www.ncba.org.

266. Email In order to send and receive email, you need a computer and a connection from your computer to a server that is in turn connected to the Internet (a federation of millions of computers in some 50,000 networks around the world.) If your organization does not offer that service, you can purchase it for a small fee from any of numerous on-line services, such as America On Line (1-888-265-8006).

Email is easy to use, inexpensive, very fast, and convenient for sending messages, reports, and files to individuals or groups. Moreover, the email messages you receive are already in a form suitable for storing or editing on your computer. It is easy to reply to an email message, and you can even interlard the original with your comments, questions and answers.

Microsoft Outlook offers excellent email capability including distribution lists for email, organizing email by folders, blind carbon copies (hidden additional recipients of the message), previews of messages, powerful tools to search among your sent and deleted messages and more.

You can spend too much time reading unnecessary email messages, especially if you are on email lists. Also email is not confidential.

267. Email clean-up Just like paper correspondence, email can pile up if not attended to.

- Email software like Microsoft Outlook lets you assign priorities to some email sources and filter out others.
- Skim through the mail accumulated in your in-box. Delete some items (you can set the display so you can see the first few lines of each message as well as the source, date, subject and priority). Move other items to other folders where you can retrieve them readily if necessary. Click on Reply for those you wish to answer.

BENEFITS

BURDENS

BALANCE

- When you receive unsolicited email, hit reply and ask to be taken off the list.
- When registering software you have purchased, do not check the box that grants permission to share your email address with other vendors.

 268. Email deletion After reading your email messages, delete them or assign them to a folder (e.g. Letters from Friends).

- When you delete email messages, you actually place them in the trash mailbox (which you can empty if you are short of space on your hard drive by selecting Empty Trash).
- If you do empty your trash, be sure to include in the list of nicknames those addresses you may need later. If you save your trash, you can search through it for email addresses.

269. Find anyone

You can find anyone and any business using the Web.

www.bigyellow.411.com
www.switchboard.com
www.eu-info.com
Reverse telephone number search: www.anywho.com
www.whowhere.com
www.worldpages.com
www.people.yahoo.com

270. Food

www.epicurious.com
www.foodwine.com
www.foodweb.com
www.foodtv.com
www.ichef.com
www.restaurantscene.com
www.yumyum.com

TIME-SAVING TIP   INFLUENCE   FOCUS

271. Government

POSTAL SERVICE www.usps.com (rate information available)
DEPT. OF VETERAN'S AFFAIRS: www.va.gov
ENVIRONMENTAL PROTECTION AGENCY: www.epa.gov
    www.fbi.gov
FEDERAL EMERGENCY MANAGEMENT AGENCY: www.fema.gov
GOVERNMENT PRINTING OFFICE: www.access.gpo.gov
HOUSING AND URBAN DEVELOPMENT: www.hud.gov
IMMIGRATION AND NATURALIZATION SERVICE:
    www.ins.usdoj.gov
INTERNAL REVENUE SERVICE: www.irs.ustreas.gov
NATIONAL SCIENCE FOUNDATION: www.nsf.gov
OCCUPATIONAL SAFETY & HEALTH ADMINISTRATION:
    www.osha.gov
PEACE CORPS: www.peacecorps.gov
SOCIAL SECURITY: www.ssa.gov
U.S. DEPT. OF COMMERCE: www.doc.gov
U.S. DEPT. OF EDUCATION: www.gopher.ed.gov
U.S. DEPT. OF HEALTH & HUMAN SERVICES: www.os.dhhs.gov
U.S. DEPT. OF LABOR: www.dol.gov
U.S. FOOD AND DRUG ADMINISTRATION: www.fda.gov
U.S. SECURITIES & EXCHANGE COMMISSION: www.sec.gov

272. Home

BETTER HOMES & GARDENS: www.bhglive.com
www.homearts.com
www.gardennet.com
www.homecentral.com
www.homedepot.com

273. Insurance

www.aetna.com
www.allstate.com
www.metlife.com
NEW ENGLAND LIFE INSURANCE: wwwtne.com
www.statefarm.com

BENEFITS

BURDENS

BALANCE

274. Medicine & Health

SEARCH MEDICAL LITERATURE:
www. Ncbi.nlm.nih.gov/pubMed
www.healthseek.com
www.shapeup.org
www.familyweb.com
www.rxlist.com
www.alcoholics-anonymous.org
NATIONAL CLEARINGHOUSE FOR ALCOHOL & DRUG
INFORMATION: www.health.org
www.alternativemedicine.com
DOC IN THE BOX: www.proservices.com
www.mentalhealth.com
MENTAL HEALTH NET: www.cmhc.com
www.foodallergy.com
www.health-net.com
www.medaccess.com
FITNESS: www.cybercise.com
www.fitnesszone.com
www.bluecares.com
www.biosupplynet.com
www.cyberdiet.com

275. Minorities

ASIAN-AMERICAN: www.asianweek.com
LATINO/A: www.latinworld.com
NATIVE AMERICAN: www.nativeamerican.org
GAY, LESBIAN: www.planetout.com; www.gaywebworld.com
AFRICAN-AMERICAN: www.afrinet.net
DEAF: www.deafworldweb.org
DISABLED PEOPLE INTERNATIONAL: www.dpi.org
SENIOR CITIZENS: www.arp.org

276. News and Entertainment

FILM REVIEWS: www.film.com
CURRENT FILMS: www.filmsite.com
INTERNET MOVIE DATABASE: www.us.imdb.com
www.abctelevision.com
www.cbs.com
www.nbc.com

TIME-SAVING TIP

INFLUENCE

FOCUS

www.cnn.com
www.pbs.org
www.bluesworld.com
www.classical.net
www.artsinfo.com
www.countrysong.com
www.contemporaryjazz.com
www.metopera.org
www.rockweb.com

277. Personal finance

www.americanexpress.com
DELOITTE & TOUCHE: www.dttus.com
www.handrblock.com
www.intuit.com
www.kiplinger.com
MERRILL LYNCH: www.ml.com
www.irs.ustreas.gov (many forms available)

278. Pets

www.aspca.org
www.acmepet.com
www.allpets.com
www.cyberpet.com

279. Reference materials

BRITTANICA ONLINE: www.eb.com
MERRIAM WEBSTER ONLINE: www.m-w.com
ROGET'S THESAURUS: www.thesaurus.com

280. Search engines To find just about anything on the Net, you can put your query to any, or several, information services, called "search engines":

www.askjeeves.com
www.metacrawler.com
www.yahoo.com
www.altavista.com

BENEFITS

BURDENS

BALANCE

www.northernlight.com
www.google.com
www.dogpile.com
www.bigbook.com
www.lycos.com
www.hotbot.com

281. Shipping

DHL WORLDWIDE EXPRESS: www.dhl.com
FEDERAL EXPRESS: www.fedex.com
UNITED PARCEL SERVICE: www.ups.com

282. Shopping

www.apparel.net
www.beautylink.com
BOOKS: (see Computers-Internet-books)
www.autobuyer.com
www.autoweb.com
BUY A NEW CAR: www.greenlight.com
www.cataloglink.com
COMPUTERS: (See Computers-Internet-hardware)
www.jcpenny.com
www.bloomingdales.com
www.kmart.com
www.macys.com
www.servicemerchandise.com
www.1-800-flowers.com
www.faoschwartz.com
www.garden.com
www.jewelrymall.com
ONLINE AUCTION: www.ebay.com
www.cdnow.com
www.officemax.com
www.internet-mall.com

283. Stocks & Bonds

Trade stocks and bonds and manage your portfolio:

www.deanwitter.com

TIME-SAVING TIP

INFLUENCE

FOCUS

MERRILL LYNCH: www.ml.com
www.painewebber.com
www.schwab.com
www.smithbarney.com
www.dowjones.com
www.goldman.com
www.investor's guide
MORGAN STANLEY: www.ms.com
www.salomon.com
STANDARD & POOR'S: www.stockinfo.standardpoor.com
www.morningstar.net
www.dreyfus.com
www.fidelity.com
www.kemper.com
www.etrade.com
www.bloomberg.com
www.dljdirect.com
www.ameritrade.com
www.etrade.com

284. Think Web Form the habit of thinking first of the ○
Internet when you need information. You will often obtain it
much more quickly than by going to a library or telephoning a col-
league. Use one of the search engines (See Computers-Internet),
enter the key words for your topic, and let the Internet serve you.

285. Travel You can select the best flights for your schedule ○
and pocket book using the Web and find maps tailored to your
needs and weather forecasts, too:

   www.fodors.com
   www.Travelocity.com
   www.travel.yahoo.com
   www.maps.yahoo.com
   www.homexchange.com
   EXCHANGE RATES: www.oanda.com/converter/classic
   WEATHER: accuwx.com; www.intellicast.com; www.usato-
      day.com/weather
   BED & BREAKFAST: www.ibbp.com
   concierge.com

BENEFITS

BURDENS

BALANCE

SOFTWARE

🕐 **286. Backup** You will certainly lose access to your computer files one day when the hard drive or its controller develops a defect—in five years from purchase on the average. If you delete a file or one becomes corrupted by accident, you will be glad you back up daily. Buy a backup device and schedule automatic backups:

- The Hewlett-Packard Colorado Systems magnetic tape drive is the least expensive solution; it is slow but if you back up automatically while you're asleep, what do you care?
- The Ricoh Mediamaster recordable CD-Rom drive is faster and has the largest capacity (640 MB). ($200; 1-877-742-6479).
- Iomega Zip 250 MB drive. ($200. 1-800-697-8833). Uses high capacity diskettes.
- Make a full backup of your entire hard drive (this can take a few hours), and then set the scheduler to daily make a backup of files that have changed since the last full backup.
- Schedule full backups weekly at a time when you know you will be away from your computer. When a backup tape or disc is full, exhaust several more before reusing the first. For example, set aside ten tape cartridges; three for weekly backups and seven for daily backups.
- As a precaution against theft, fire or flood, keep one full backup in another location and update it monthly or more often.

🕐 **287. Compatibility** Before you buy software, look on the box: Do you have the operating system, and more than the required amount of memory and space on your hard disk? Do you have a compatible processor and video card? Don't cut it too close—manufacturers understate their requirements to increase sales.

If you are buying communications software, for example, to send and receive faxes, be sure that the modem in your computer is compatible. Also ask about conflicts and compatibility among the software packages you will be using. For example, MS

TIME-SAVING TIP

INFLUENCE

FOCUS

Word will not access Delrina Winfax address books, and Delrina will not access the address book in the MS Personal Information Manager called Outlook.

288. Desktop If you have several windows open and need to get to the desktop, right click the task bar in a blank area and select *minimize all windows*. Windows Internet Explorer also places a *show desktop* icon on the task bar. Finally, if you have a windows compatible keyboard, you can reach the desktop by touching the key with the windows icon and then the letter *m*.

289. Desktop Put on your desktop shortcuts to the most common MS Word templates you use. To do this, click on *File in MS Word*, then *New*. Right click on a template that you use; click on *create shortcut*. Reduce the window so the desk top is visible. Click on the new shortcut icon and drag it onto the desktop.

If you use Microsoft Office, you can save space on your desktop by customizing your Office shortcut bar.

290. Documents One of the blessings of the computer operating system Windows 95 and its successors is that they allow you to assign lengthy explicit names, including spaces, to each file that you create. For example, you can call your list of people who sent you Christmas cards (you do keep track, don't you?) *People who sent Christmas cards* 2000.

291. File management Discard old computer files and programs on your hard disk that are no longer needed. See the caution below.

- If your word processing software makes backup copies of all the files you save, you can delete those, especially if you backup regularly. (See Computers-Software-Backup.)
- Use the Windows Explorer or File Manager programs that come with Windows 95 and successors to view the contents of a directory you want to clean up. Select files that are adjacent in the list for one pass deletion by holding down the shift key and clicking on the first and last with your mouse.

BENEFITS   BURDENS   BALANCE

Nonadjacent files can be deleted at once by holding down the control key while selecting the files to be deleted.

- You can take Windows programs that you never use off your disk with the help of a program such as Quarterdeck's Clean Sweep. After housecleaning, remember to defragment your disk. (See Computers-Hardware-Maintenance.)
- Before you delete a program, check to see if it is listed in *Add/Remove programs* (Start>Settings>Control Panel). If it is, select it and click on *Remove* there; do not delete it in any other way!
- Check *Start>Programs* and the name of the program you wish to delete for a companion uninstall program. If you have one, use the uninstall program. It will find and delete numerous fragments of your program that are scattered under various directories.

👍 More space on your disk; easier to search for files.

👎 Time to clean the disk; danger of discarding something needed later (see our tips on file retrieval and backup).

🕐 **292. File organization** When saving a file, always save it into an appropriate folder such as *faxes, letters to Mom*, etc. If no appropriate folder has been set up, create one yourself with Windows Explorer. Feel free to create folders within folders so your files stay organized, and you don't have too many documents at any one level.

🕐 **293. File retrieval** We urge you to delete files that are no longer needed. However, occasionally you delete a file and then realize you needed it after all. To be sure you will be able to retrieve deleted files, right click on the recycle bin (desktop), click on properties, and allocate 10 percent of your disk space for deleted files. Set the purge delay to a week (or longer if appropriate).

🕐 **294. Manuals** When you buy new software, you may begrudge the time it takes to read the operating instructions on the screen or in the manual. Do it sooner or later, though, or you

TIME-SAVING TIP

INFLUENCE

FOCUS

will miss helpful features and waste time solving problems you could have avoided. You will probably not be able to absorb all the important information in one pass, so review the instructions after you have had some experience with the software.

295. Printer access If you put the printer's icon on the desktop, you can print documents by dragging their icons onto the printer icon. To put the printer icon on your desktop, click on My Computer, then on Printers. Right-click on your printer icon, click on create shortcut, click and hold on the shortcut, and drag it onto the desktop.

If you send a file to the printer by mistake, you can click on the icon you just created and purge the pages waiting to be printed.

296. Shortcuts Learn the shortcuts for many computer functions. It is often easier to make a couple of keystrokes than to grasp and position a mouse. To see which strokes to use, position the mouse over the icon, or click on the drop-down menu.

297. Taskbar If you need access to several folders or pieces of software concurrently, such as email and word processing, you can arrange to have those applications open automatically each time you start up your computer. Using Windows Explorer, drag the icons for those programs onto *Windows\Start Menu\Programs\Startup*. These icons will appear on the task bar at the right.

You can also put icons on the task bar at the left for quick (single-click) launching. Since the task bar is always visible while the desktop is not, this will save you some more clicks. With Windows Explorer, copy the icons for the software programs you want to quick launch (these have the suffix *.exe*) onto this folder: *\Windows\Application Data\Microsoft\Internet Explorer\Quick Launch*. Launching windows and those programs can take a maddeningly long time; have a cup of coffee, read your mail, or just leave your computer on all the time; we do. (You will want to leave it on anyway if you use your computer to receive faxes or voice-mail. There is merit, however, in restarting your computer occasionally, to clear system memory and temporary files.)

BENEFITS

BURDENS

BALANCE

A very helpful feature of Windows is the *Tile Windows Horizontally or Vertically* in order to view multiple application windows at a time. With at least two applications open, right-click on the *task bar*. Tiling facilitates transferring information from one file to the other: Paint the source selection, click on it, and drag it from the source to the destination. If you want to leave the original in the source, hold down the *shift* key before dragging.

 298. Tech Support Unfortunately, you are going to need to contact tech support. When you call, you are likely to confront tedious menu choices, a long wait on hold, and an ill-informed technician with a high-handed manner. Tech support services generally do not call you back when they say they will. And they have recently started charging a lot of money.

- Don't buy a computer or a crucial piece of software without trying to reach their tech support at a few different times to see how long it takes.
- Write the tech support number and the menu choice numbers you must dial when you call where you can find them readily, along with the serial number of the product you are using, and essential information about your computer and operating system.
- Find out tech support hours in the time zone where they are located (those are usually in their recording or in the manual) and call exactly as they open. Avoid calling Monday morning, when others are calling who encountered problems during the weekend.
- If you do get to speak with tech support ask them for the days and times it is best to call.
- Since you will surely have to wait, call using a speakerphone and have busy-work handy.
- Tech support wants to tell you what you need to know and go on to the next customer; however, it is in your interest to learn as much as possible from the contact, especially as it is so hard to achieve. Prepare a list of questions and ask at the end if there is anything more you need to know, anything you failed to ask about but should have.
- If you are not in a rush to solve your problem, try using the Internet to put your questions to tech support (see our tips in Internet-Computers). Microsoft has a free Web Response for licensed

TIME-SAVING TIP

INFLUENCE

FOCUS

products found under their tech support section. (Website: http://support.microsoft.com/support/contact/default.asp)

299. Templates
Many word processing programs allow you to create "templates" for the different kinds of documents you prepare, such as memos, letters, and articles. The template contains all that is constant in the document type, including your name and address (if you wish), a standard closing, etc. It also contains all the settings you have chosen such as font and point, margins, spacing, and the like.

If you are using MS Word, change directory to \templates\. Select *open document template;* make changes to suit your needs and save as a new template with the *.dot* extension. Then create a shortcut and put the icon on the desktop.

300. Time trap
Computers save you a lot of time, but they can also be a time trap: You can invest too much time in finding, purchasing, installing and learning to use software and hardware, so that your net gain in time thanks to the computer is much reduced.

Try to build a relationship with a friend or professional person who stays abreast of computer hardware and software of the type you use and who won't mind receiving frantic calls at all hours of the day and night. He or she can help you solve problems and alert you to new products.

301. Update
Do not systematically buy the new version or upgrade of a program if you are happy with the one you use now. Buying, installing, troubleshooting, and mastering the upgrade may take more time than it's worth if the new features are not useful for you.

302. Virus
The list of viruses that can invade your hard disk through email, the Internet, or diskettes from others and do great harm grows longer daily. To protect yourself:

- Backup regularly and keep old backups at least one week.

BENEFITS

BURDENS

BALANCE

- Buy anti-virus protection (e.g., Norton AntiVirus: 1 800-441-7324); use the Internet to keep the software up-to-date so it detects the newest viruses.
- Set the security protection on your Internet browser.
- Be cautious in inserting diskettes that are not from a software manufacturer.
- Do not open email or email attachments from a source you do not recognize.

 303. Word processors Use autocorrect in MS Word and other word processing software. To avoid repetitive typing, insert such phrases in the list under *Autocorrect* in *Tools*. Click on *automatic insertion*, then on *add*. When you type the key words, a bubble will invite you to confirm the completion which will be done for you.

TIME-SAVING TIP   INFLUENCE   FOCUS

Food

PREPARATION

304. Cakes Rather good cakes and pies can be found in super- 🕐
markets and bakeries. And there are frozen pies you can pop into the
oven. Do you really want to spend the time making your own from
scratch?

⚖️ Home made is more delicious and, besides, the children can pitch
in and learn from the experience.

305. Canned food The flavor and texture of some foods sur- 🕐
vive the canning process (for example, baked beans) but most foods
lose their flavor as well as some of their nutritional value. Prefer
frozen foods, which can be quickly prepared with a microwave oven.

306. Crock pot Put some food in an electric "crock pot"
when you leave in the morning; a warm tasty dish will be ready 🕐
when you return.

307. Doubling up Don't hesitate to prepare dishes that are
slow to cook, provided they don't tie you down. For example, you 🕐
can prepare a roast beef by inserting the roast in the oven at high

heat, shutting off the oven a half hour later, and allowing the roast to go on cooking as the oven cools. You are free to spend almost all of that time elsewhere.

For slow stovetop cooking, buy a flame tamer, a metal disk that sits on top of a gas burner and reduces the flame's intensity. A pot of soup can simmer at very low heat and needs only minimal attention.

308. Fast food Here is a list of dishes that are fast to prepare

SNACKS
Cereal
Chili (prepared)
Granola bars
Hamburgers
Hotdogs
Lox and bagels
Melted cheese sandwich
Omelets
Pizza
Popcorn
Quesadilla (tortilla with melted cheese)
Salmon paté
Sandwiches
Soup
Tacos

MAIN DISHES
Beef & broccoli stir-fry
Chicken breast, broiled
Chicken, roasted with baked potatoes
Ham steak, broiled
Pork chops, broiled
Scallops and pasta (use prepared pasta from refrigerator case)
Spaghetti & meatballs
Steak grilled
Stuffed peppers
Tuna casserole

DESSERTS

TIME-SAVING TIP   INFLUENCE   FOCUS

Cakes
Cookies
Frozen yogurt
Fruit
Ice cream
Pies
Puddings

 Sometimes, time pressure is so great that a fast meal is your best choice; preparation and eating at home is often faster than going to a restaurant or cafeteria.

If you restrict yourself to preparing fast foods, you will miss out on much good nutrition and dining pleasure.

Even though food is prepared quickly, it can look and taste delicious and you do not need to hurry through the meal.

309. Fast meals There are many dinner menus that take relatively little of your time. These include: broiled hamburger; spaghetti and sauce; broiled fish; and frozen pizza.

Some dishes require time in the oven, but you can set the oven timer and turn to other things: broiled chicken; roast beef. If you use the oven, slip in some baked potatoes. Numerous frozen vegetables are available to complement these dishes and they are quickly prepared in the microwave. A salad is quickly prepared (and prepackaged mixed green salads are increasingly available). Fruit, cookies, ice cream round off the quick-preparation meal.

In the section Food-Recipes we offer a selection of American and French main dishes that are quick to prepare (20 minutes or less) and delicious to eat. The French recipes come from the leading French authority on food, Jean-Pierre Coffe, and have been adapted to American products and measures. (Co-author Christian Wayser was Jean-Pierre Coffe's collaborator for daily TV and radio shows, as well as numerous books and CD-ROMS.)

Fast need not mean nasty; buy fresh quality products—lean beef, good cuts of meat, fresh fish, good rolls or bread—and enjoy your meals!

BENEFITS   BURDENS   BALANCE

310. Food processor Use the slicer blade of your food processor to shred lettuce, or cabbage or slice cheese or cucumber. The chopping blade will chop onion, dice ham or mash avocado. Sirloin will be easy to slice if you keep it in the freezer about a ½ hour.

Chop vegetables in bulk that you will use throughout the week; keep in the refrigerator in sealable plastic storage bags or plastic containers. Most should keep for up to a week.

311. Infant formula Use a microwave oven to heat or reheat baby bottles on demand; they will reach the perfect temperature in seconds.

312. Large pot Use a larger pot than necessary to avoid food boiling over.

313. Microwave cooking Most vegetables, whether frozen or fresh, cook faster and taste better when prepared in a microwave oven. Check Consumer Reports for the latest features and prices.

Have you ever eaten fresh peas that have simmered slowly in a buttered pan? Remember how those aromas made your mouth water?

314. Salad dryer You can make a delicious salad in a snap with pre-washed and packaged mixed greens of various kinds; slice in a tomato, some celery, carrots and radishes if you wish, add low-fat dressing and enjoy!

If you prefer to buy a head of lettuce, or other greens that need washing, consider buying a salad dryer—a perforated bowl that forces the water out into a larger container as you spin it. The dryer can be used to store the salad until you are ready to add dressing.

315. Teach your children
Teach your children—both girls and boys—how to cook. Once they have mastered some skills, their collaboration can save

TIME-SAVING TIP

INFLUENCE

FOCUS

you time and make the task more enjoyable—and they'll be grateful for the knowledge and skills which will serve them for the rest of their lives.

316. Tips:

- To peel tomatoes easily and quickly, put them into boiling water for roughly one minute or until the first sign that the skin has split, then plunge into cold water.
- To remove the skin of frozen fish, freeze it. Then hold it under hot water for a few seconds, and peel.
- Don't waste time pounding your steaks to tenderize them: ask your butcher to use a tenderizer.
- For fast and easy frying, use a wok.
- When oven baking or roasting, line the pan with aluminum foil for faster clean up.

317. TV dinners
Tear, puncture, wave, chomp—that's all it takes to prepare and consume a TV dinner. Keep a few in the freezer for those times when there's no time to eat, never mind prepare food.

If you boil some chicken breasts and store them in your freezer, you could prepare a nice salad with chicken in about the same time as a frozen dinner.

Don't do this too often; dining is one of life's pleasures.

RECIPES

318. About our recipes
We focus on the main course; if you're in a hurry that's all you will eat. Nearly all of these dishes can be prepared in 20 minutes or less. (A food processor will speed up slicing, chopping, mixing etc.)

If you wish begin with a salad—most stores now have a wide variety of delicious mixed greens in a bag—or other prepared appetizers. Follow the main course with store-bought desserts or

BENEFITS

BURDENS

BALANCE

sherbets or ice cream from your freezer. All the recipes are for four people; if you are two people, divide quantities by two, if one person, divide by four. Always add salt and pepper to taste.

The French recipes (tips 364–377) are adapted from recipes provided by French food authority, Jean-Pierre Coffe. (Co-author Christian Wayser was Jean-Pierre Coffe's collaborator for daily TV and radio shows, as well as numerous books and CD-ROMS.)

⏱ 319. Blazing Burritos

1. Warm tortillas, then pour ½ cup hot canned chili onto each.
2. Top with shredded lettuce, shredded cheddar or Monterey Jack cheese, and diced tomato. Fold in ends and sides, and serve.

⏱ 320. Brisk Beef Stir-fry

1. Bring a can of beef broth to a boil and stir in 1 cup couscous (precooked semolina); remove from heat.
2. Slice 1½ lbs boneless sirloin into ¼ -inch thick strips and stir-fry in hot skillet with 3 tablespoons of olive oil (1-2 minutes); keep warm.
3. In same skillet fry 1 pepper cut into strips, and 1 sliced sweet onion 2 or 3 minutes. Add the steak and pour ½ cup barbecue sauce of choice over it. Cook 1 or 2 minutes and serve.

⏱ 321. Bullet Train Chicken

1. Mix an 8 ½ oz jar of chutney with an 8-oz can of drained crushed pineapple, add 1 tablespoon of curry powder and pour over 4 chicken-breast halves.
2. Broil for 5 minutes on each side and serve.

⏱ 322. Chicken Enchilada

1. Preheat oven to 350°F.
2. Brown ½ lb skinless boneless chicken-breast halves over medium heat with a little peanut or canola oil. Sprinkle with ½ teaspoon each of garlic powder and cumin, and

 TIME-SAVING TIP   INFLUENCE   FOCUS

cook seven 7 minutes per side). Add ¼ cup of chicken broth, remove chicken and let cool.

3. Sauté ½ a medium-sized chopped onion in 1 tablespoon of olive oil, then add ½ a sixteen-oz can of stewed tomatoes, a 7-oz can of green chilies diced, ½ cup thawed corn, ¼ teaspoon Mexican spice mix; cook for 1 minute.

4. Shred chicken and add to skillet. Spoon chicken mixture over 4 warm tortillas over filling, place in baking pan with seam-side down. Top with enchilada sauce and cheese.

5. Bake until cheese has melted and browned in spots (10–15 minutes).

323. Chicken in a Flash ⏱

1. Wrap a strip of uncooked bacon around each of 4 chicken-breast halves in a baking dish.

2. Broil each side for 5 minutes or until done (turn once). Salt and pepper to taste.

324. Chicken Now ⏱

1. Cut 4 chicken breasts into strips and simmer for 10 minutes in a saucepan with a cup or so of water and place in baking dish.

2. In a mixing bowl, stir 2 cups flour, 1 beaten egg, 3 tablespoons oil, and add ice water until doughy. Roll small pieces into bite-sized balls and drop into 1 cup simmering chicken broth, cooking until broth thickens

3. When cooked, pour dumplings and broth over chicken. Cover with prepared pie-dough crust and bake at 425°F until crust is golden (30 minutes).

325. Cod at a Clip ⏱

1. Cut a 1½-lb cod fillet into 4 pieces, dip each piece in flour, and cook in a skillet until done for 5 minutes on each side over medium-high heat.

2. Chop a cucumber and a half-dozen radishes, squeeze excess liquid from cucumber, add 3 tablespoons of mayonnaise and 1 tablespoon white wine vinegar and pour over cod.

BENEFITS

BURDENS

BALANCE

🕐 326. Cyclone Cajun Shrimp

1. Thaw or defrost 1½-lbs of frozen shrimp (shelled, deveined) in the microwave oven.
2. Mix 2 teaspoons of paprika, 1 teaspoon each of dried thyme and garlic powder, ½ teaspoon each of salt, cayenne pepper, garlic powder, and a good pinch of nutmeg, and coat shrimp with the mixture.
3. Cook spiced shrimp over medium-high heat, gently stirring, for about 3 minutes.

🕐 327. Express Asparagus

1. Heat water for pasta.
2. Cook one 10-oz package of asparagus tips in a skillet over medium-high heat with 3 tablespoons of olive oil for 4 minutes.
3. Boil 1 lb pasta following directions on the package, drain, replace in pot, add the asparagus and olive oil, salt and pepper, stir, and serve.

🕐 328. Fast Flank Steak

1. Rub a 1 ½-lb beef flank steak with a mixture of 1 teaspoon of chili powder and 1 teaspoon of dark-brown sugar, 2 tablespoons of lime juice, and 3 finely chopped garlic cloves or 1 teaspoon of garlic powder.
2. Surround with onion wedges and broil until done (7 minutes/side).

🕐 329. Fleet Poached Salmon

1. Cook a package of frozen rice and peas in the microwave; add 2 tablespoons of butter and set aside.
2. Place four 6-oz salmon fillets (or other fish from cod to red snapper) in a microwave able baking dish with ¼ cup dry white wine, cover and cook on high for 6 minutes. Drain salmon on paper towels. Serve with the rice and peas.

 TIME-SAVING TIP   INFLUENCE   FOCUS

330. Galloping Ginger

1. Marinate 2 salmon fillets (½ lb each) in ¼ cup white wine vinegar and 2 tablespoons of soy sauce and let sit.
2. Mix 2 tablespoons horseradish, ½ cup bread crumbs, and 1 tablespoon fresh ginger root in mini-chopper or food processor and chop finely.
3. Spread the mixture over the salmon and bake for 30 minutes at 375° F.

331. Greyhound Grilled Chicken

1. Broil a 2½-lb quartered chicken for 15 minutes, add four precooked bratwurst sausages (scored) and broil 10 minutes more or until chicken is done, brushing repeatedly with a mixture of ½ cup of marmalade and 2 tablespoons of fresh lemon juice.

332. Hasty Chicken

1. Flour four boneless chicken-breast halves and brown in an olive-oiled skillet over medium-high heat.
2. Add a 14-oz can of drained sliced artichoke hearts and 1 tablespoon of lemon juice. Cook until the chicken is done.

333. Hell-bent Pizza

1. Preheat oven to 450° F. Cut a loaf of Italian or French bread crosswise into 6-inch segments. Slice each segment in half lengthwise.
2. Place on cookie sheet crust down and grill until golden.
3. Mix ½ cup whipped cream cheese, 2 tablespoons of drained and chopped capers, and 4 tablespoons of minced onion, and spread on crust. Add 8 ozs of smoked salmon cut into bite-sized pieces.

BENEFITS BURDENS BALANCE

⏱ 334. Hurried Ham

1. Thaw or defrost a package of frozen peas and a package of small white onions in the microwave oven (about 5 minutes).
2. In a skillet with a little olive oil, brown 1 ½ lbs sliced ham cut into ⅓-inch thick strips. Add vegetables and ½ teaspoon each of dried sweet basil, salt, and black pepper.
3. Cook ham, peas, and onion over medium heat for about 5 minutes.

⏱ 335. Leapin' Lamb Chops

1. Rub eight rib lamp chops (1¾-lb) with a teaspoon of dried crushed rosemary leaves and coat lightly (too much and the oil will catch fire) with olive oil. Place in baking dish.
2. Broil 5 minutes on each side.

⏱ 336. Lickety-split Linguine

1. Prepare ¾ lb of linguine following instructions on package.
2. Sauté a medium-sized onion in about 5 minutes in 2 tablespoons of olive oil. Stir in bottled clam juice (8 oz) and 2 teaspoons of garlic powder. Bring to a boil.
3. Add 1 tablespoon cornstarch blended with 2 tablespoons water and simmer for 1 minute. Add 2 lbs fresh chopped clams (or 1 10-oz can of clams perked up with 2 tablespoons of lemon juice), drained. Heat to boiling point, and pour over linguine, and serve.

⏱ 337. Lightning Lemon Chicken

1. Mix ¼ cup each white wine vinegar, lemon juice and Dijon-style mustard, then pour over 4 chicken breasts, and marinate in the refrigerator overnight.
2. Broil until done (4 minutes/side).

⏱ 338. Minute Moroccan Couscous

1. Add sliced dried figs or apricots to a cup and a half of chicken broth and bring to a boil.

TIME-SAVING TIP   INFLUENCE   FOCUS

2. Stir in a cup of couscous (precooked semolina) and 4 table-spoons chopped fresh parsley or cilantro leaves. Remove from heat and serve.

339. Momentary Meatballs

1. Preheat oven to 400° F. Spray baking sheet with nonstick spray.
2. Mix in a bowl: 1 ½ lbs lean ground beef, 2 eggs lightly beaten, ⅓ cup of dry bread crumbs, ½ smallish onion chopped fine, and 2 teaspoons of minced garlic, or ½ teaspoon garlic powder.
3. Mix and shape into meatballs, place on baking sheet and roast 10–15 minutes.

340. Plunging Pork Medallions

1. Boil water for 2 cups of couscous (precooked semolina).
2. Cut each of 2 pork tenderloins (¾ lb each) into 4 pieces crosswise and pound them with the flat of a carving knife into ½ -inch thick medallions.
3. Mix 1 teaspoon olive oil, ½ teaspoon each of dried thyme, ground cinnamon, ground black pepper, and ¼ teaspoon each of nutmeg and ground cloves.
4. Add pork and toss, then cook in skillet over medium-high heat for 5 minutes on each side. Remove from heat.
5. Add ¼ cup red-currant jelly to skillet, stirring until melted, then add ⅔ cup chicken broth and bring heat to a boil. Pour over pork and serve.

341. Presto Shrimp Pasta

1. Bring water for angel's-hair pasta or thin spaghetti to a boil.
2. Thaw or defrost 1½ lbs of frozen shrimp (shelled, de-veined) in the microwave. Cook the shrimp in a skillet with a little olive oil (about 3 minutes).
3. Slice up and cook 2 peppers in a skillet.
4. Cook 1 lb pasta following directions on package, drain it, replace it in the pot, add shrimp and peppers, and a 7-oz jar of pesto with basil. Stir and serve.

BENEFITS

BURDENS

BALANCE

342. Prompt Pork

Put some olive oil, ½ teaspoon of cayenne pepper, 1 teaspoon of garlic powder and 1 tablespoon of soy sauce in a skillet; add 1 ½ lbs of pork tenderloin cut into ¼-inch thick slices. Cook whole mixture for 10 minutes over medium heat.

343. Puttanesca Pronto

1. Prepare 1 lb corkscrew (fuselli) pasta.
2. Concurrently, mix 3 tablespoons of capers (drained, chopped), 3 tablespoons of finely chopped green onions, 2 tablespoons of red-wine vinegar, 1 can (6 oz) tuna in olive oil, 2 bunches watercress (without stems).
3. Add ½ cup pasta cooking water, stir, pour over drained pasta.

344. Quick Quesadillas

1. Brown ½ lb thinly sliced chorizo sausage or pepperoni in an oiled skillet over medium-high heat (5 minutes).
2. Sprinkle ½ lb shredded Monterey Jack cheese over 4 warm soft tortillas, arrange chorizo slices, cover with 4 more tortillas.
3. Heat these quesadillas in another skillet until golden brown and cheese has melted, turning once (5 minutes). Slice into wedges, serve with salsa and sour cream.

345. Racing Roast Pork

1. Heat oven to 400° F.
2. Brush 1 ½ lb pork tenderloins with mustard. Roast 35 to 40 minutes.
3. Concurrently, cook frozen vegetables of choice in microwave.

346. Rocket Kabobs

1. Thaw or defrost in the microwave a package of frozen peas and add to 2 cups of cooked rice (with ½ teaspoon turmeric mixed in) during the last 10 minutes of cooking. Preheat broiler.

TIME-SAVING TIP   INFLUENCE   FOCUS

2. Mix 1 tablespoon of chili powder, of soy sauce and of peanut oil with 1 teaspoon of Tabasco or jalapeno sauce. Coat beef chunks (1½ lbs sirloin cut into 1-inch cubes).
3. Skewer cubes; alternately skewer cherry tomatoes, mushrooms, segments of 3 green onions, 1 inch squares of ¾ lb zucchini. Broil skewers close to heat for 10 minutes, serve over peas and rice.

347. Salmon Penne Pronto

1. Prepare 1 lb of penne following instructions on package.
2. Concurrently, fry ⅔ lb trimmed asparagus cut into 2-in lengths in a skillet with a little olive oil for 5 minutes over high heat; add 1 minced onion, cook 2 more minutes, stirring. Add ¼ cup dry white wine, heat to boiling.
3. Add ⅔ cup chicken broth and bring back to boil.
4. Add 1 ½ lbs of cubed salmon fillet. Cover and simmer 2-3 minutes. Drain pasta, return to pot, and add the skillet contents, stir, and serve.

348. Salmon Sprint

1. Prepare 1 lb pasta following instructions on package.
2. Concurrently, bring ⅓ cup dry white wine and 1 cup light cream to a boil and simmer for 3 minutes.
3. Remove from heat and add strips of smoked salmon (½ lb). Pour over drained pasta and stir.

349. Salmon with Dill Dispatch

1. Mix 2 tablespoons each fresh dill, lemon juice, and drained chopped capers and 1 can of anchovies.
2. Brush the mixture over the flesh side of a 2-lb salmon filet; broil each side for 5 minutes. Serve with fresh dill and lemon wedges.

BENEFITS

BURDENS

BALANCE

350. Scrod Skedaddle

1. Preheat oven to 450° F.
2. Cook 1 smallish sliced onion until golden (about 8 minutes) in a skillet over medium heat with 2 tablespoon water and a little olive oil.
3. Add 1 28-oz can of drained and quartered plum tomatoes, ¼ cup red wine vinegar, and 1 tablespoon of dark-brown sugar. Cook over high heat until sauce thickens (15 minutes).
4. Put scrod filet in baking dish along with ground pepper, salt, and olive oil. Roast for 10 to 15 minutes. Pour sauce over scrod and serve.

351. Shortcut Chicken

1. Slice 2 bell peppers, 1 onion, ¼ lb mushrooms and sauté in skillet with a little olive oil (3–4 minutes) over medium heat. Set contents aside.
2. In the same pan sauté a 3-lb chicken cut up into 8 pieces (4 minutes/side). Return vegetables to pan, and add a 28-oz jar of pasta sauce. Cook over moderate heat for 25 minutes.

352. Short-lived Stir-fry Beef

1. Slice 1 ½ lbs of minute steak into ½-inch-wide strips and quickly brown in a very hot skillet with a little olive oil, then remove.
2. Cook 2 chopped red onions for a minute in the skillet, add 2 cups of beef broth and bring to boil. Add 1 ½ cups instant barley. Cover and simmer until barley is tender and liquid is absorbed. Place steak on barley and serve.

353. Short-order Scallops

1. Stir ⅔ cup of couscous (precooked semolina) into a cup of boiling water, remove from heat.
2. Defrost a package of frozen peas and microwave them following directions on package.
3. Slice an onion and a pepper and ½ lb mushrooms, and fry them for 3 minutes or so at medium heat in a skillet with a little olive oil. Remove.

 TIME-SAVING TIP   INFLUENCE   FOCUS

4. Add more olive oil to the skillet and 1½ lbs of sea scallops and sauté 3 to 5 minutes.
5. Return the vegetables to the skillet, add the peas and 2 tablespoons soy sauce; heat through and serve.

354. Shrimp Scamper

1. Defrost about 1½ lbs of uncooked shrimp in microwave.
2. Cover with an inch of beer and microwave until done (about 5 minutes). Season to taste and serve.

355. Speedy Beef Caesar

1. Broil a 1 lb flank steak.
2. Concurrently, tear up 2 heads of different kinds of lettuce into bite-size pieces. Add prepared Caesar salad dressing (or mix 2 tablespoons each of olive oil, mayonnaise, grated parmesan cheese, and 1 tablespoon each of mustard, lemon juice, and garlic powder and a teaspoon of anchovy paste).
3. Slice steak thinly and toss with salad. Sprinkle with more Parmesan. Salt, pepper to taste.

356. Split-second Shrimp

1. Thaw or defrost ½ lb frozen shrimp (shelled, deveined) in a microwave oven.
2. Meanwhile, slice a small eggplant cross-wise into ¼-inch thick rounds, brush with olive oil, and broil until brown (5 minutes/side).
3. Cook the shrimp in a skillet with a little olive oil and 2 teaspoons of finely chopped garlic or 1 of garlic powder (about 3 minutes).
4. Add a 16-oz can of drained white beans and 1 cup water and 1 tablespoon of flour. Bring to a boil and pour over eggplant.

BENEFITS

BURDENS

BALANCE

⏱ 357. Step-on-it Steak au Poivre

1. Coat both sides of four filet mignon steaks (1 in thick, 4 oz each) with black cracked pepper and salt, cook in an oiled skillet 8-10 minutes over high heat and remove steaks from skillet.
2. Add ¼ cup brandy (set aflame, but avert your eyes and hold the skillet at arm's length), then 1 tablespoon of Dijon-style mustard to skillet and stir.
3. Bring to boiling point and simmer 2 minutes. Pour the sauce over the steaks and serve.

⏱ 358. Streaking Swordfish

1. Broil 1 ¼ lb of swordfish cut into four pieces, 5 minutes/side.
2. Concurrently, heat one 14 ½-oz can of plum tomatoes; drain.
3. Place swordfish on top of canned tomatoes and sprinkle with ¼ cup crumbled feta cheese, 2 chopped cloves of garlic or ¼ teaspoon garlic powder, ¼ cup pitted ripe olives, 1 chopped fresh tomato, and broil until cheese is melted, and serve.

⏱ 359. Sudden Ceviche

1. In a serving bowl, set 2 lbs of scallops, mackerel, or any fresh fish without bones and suitable for sushi, cut into bite-sized pieces. Add ¾ of a cup of lime juice. Cover and refrigerate overnight or at least 1 hour.
2. Drain serving bowl; add 2 cups of diced tomatoes, ½ cup minced onion, 2 chopped jalapeno peppers or chilies Serrano's, 3 tablespoons of chopped cilantro, and 2 tablespoons of olive oil. Toss, and serve on 2 cups of shredded lettuce.

⏱ 360. Supersonic Pork Chops

1. Cook 1 thinly sliced medium-size onion over low heat in a covered skillet from 5 to 10 minutes.
2. Cook 4 boneless pork chops, turning several times, in a large skillet with a little olive oil over medium-high heat for 10 to 15 minutes.

TIME-SAVING TIP

INFLUENCE

FOCUS

3. Meanwhile, cut an apple into ¼-inch thick slices and brown in 1 tablespoon of olive oil in the skillet over medium heat. Remove to a serving dish with pork chops and onion.
4. In a small saucepan, blend ½ cup of apple juice with 1 tablespoon of cornstarch and heat to boiling. Add to the dish with the apple-onion-pork chop mixture, and serve.

361. Swift Shrimp

1. Thaw 1 ½ lbs of frozen shrimp. Start water boiling for pasta, add 1 lb pasta, boil for approximately 10 minutes (follow package instructions).
2. Add 1 cup of peas and the shrimp to the pasta and water. Boil over medium-high heat for 3 minutes. Drain and replace in pot.
3. Add salt and pepper, 1 chopped garlic clove, 3 diced tomatoes, 2 tablespoons olive oil, and ½ cup crumbled feta cheese. Heat, stirring, and serve.

362. Tear-Along Turkey

1. Blend 2 tablespoons lime juice, ¼ cup plain yogurt, 1 teaspoon of grated fresh ginger root, ½ teaspoon each cumin, coriander, salt, garlic powder.
2. Coat 1½ lbs turkey cutlets with this mixture, then broil until done (4 minutes on each side).

363. Tuna Burgers

1. Finely chop 1 ½ lb tuna steak.
2. Add 2 tablespoons of soy sauce, 1 teaspoon of grated fresh ginger, and pepper to taste. Shape patties with your hands and dip in ¼ cup of dry bread crumbs and 2 tablespoons of sesame seeds.
3. Brown in skillet with 3 tablespoons of olive oil over medium heat for six to eight minutes.

BENEFITS

BURDENS

BALANCE

364. Broiled Chicken à la Diable

1. Combine 1 beaten egg with 1 tablespoon of olive oil, a generous pinch of herbs of Provence, a tablespoon of Dijon-style mustard and coat chicken legs.
2. Put 4 chicken legs in cold oven and raise temperature to 200° F for 30 minutes, then raise temperature to 350° F for 15 minutes, and finally to 400° F until skin is golden and crusty. Baste the chicken legs regularly throughout with 4 tablespoons of melted butter.

365. Butter Sole

1. Lightly flour 2 lbs of sole.
2. Cook sole in 3 tablespoons of canola oil for 3 minutes per side over high heat. Remove and pat fish with a paper towel.
3. Melt 8 tablespoons of butter in a heavy-bottomed saucepan along with the juice of 1 lemon and salt and pepper. Whip until foamy.
4. Coat fish with this sauce, sprinkle with 2 tablespoons of chopped parsley, and serve.

366. Cheese Fondue

1. Reduce ¾ cup dry white wine mixed with 1 chopped garlic clove by boiling down to ⅔ cup (use microwave).
2. Strain out garlic. Chop 1 ½ cups Swiss cheese in food processor. Mix cheese with 1 tablespoon flour. Cut bread into 1-inch cubes.
3. Bring reduced wine to a simmer in enameled saucepan or fondue pot, adding cheese while stirring until a smooth creamy mass results.
4. Blend in 1 tablespoon of butter and 1–3 tablespoons heavy cream. Season with salt and pepper, and add 2 tablespoons Kirsch liqueur. Serve with French or Italian bread.

367. Chicken au Curry

1. Heat 2 tablespoons of canola or peanut oil and 2 of butter in a pot. Add 1 chicken cut into twelve pieces by butcher.
2. Cover and cook over low heat for 15–20 minutes. Remove

TIME-SAVING TIP

INFLUENCE

FOCUS

chicken and put in baking dish, cover with aluminum foil, and put in slow oven to keep hot.

3. Chop 2 large onions, and cook in covered pot over low heat for 15 minutes until brown and transparent.
4. Simmer chicken in the pot with ½ cup of chicken broth for 15 minutes.
5. Meanwhile, in a saucepan, bring 3 oz heavy cream with 1 teaspoon of curry to a boil and simmer for 3 minutes. Strain the sauce onto the chicken, decorate with a few raisins. Serve with rice or sautéed mushrooms.

368. Chicken Brochettes

1. Cut 2 lbs of chicken breasts with skin into brochette-size pieces and skewer.
2. Baste the brochettes with 1 tablespoon of cognac. Sprinkle them with 1 tablespoon of paprika. Flour the brochettes.
3. Heat 2 tablespoons of butter and 3 tablespoons of olive oil in a skillet. Brown the brochettes for a few minutes until they become a bit crusty.
5. Put the brochettes in oven at 350° F for 15 minutes. Serve with tartar sauce. (Crush the yolks of 2 hard-boiled eggs and 1 ½ tablespoon of white wine vinegar in a bowl to form a smooth paste. Mix 3 tablespoons of chopped chives and 3 of mayonnaise and blend with ¼ cup of olive oil.)

369. Chicken Wings with Sherry

1. Use 6 chicken wings or 4 chicken-breast halves with skin removed and cut into small strips.
2. Put 2 tablespoons of butter in a pot and cook chicken over low heat for 10 minutes. Remove chicken.
3. Brown ¾ lb of quartered mushrooms for 3–4 minutes in the pot.
4. Skim off fat and add ¼ cup of dry sherry. Boil to reduce by half.
5. Add a cup of heavy cream. Simmer for 6–7 minutes.
6. Add 12 chopped pitted black olives and 1 teaspoon of Dijon-style mustard and blend with a whisk.
7. Add chicken and simmer for 2–3 minutes. Serve with rice or pasta.

BENEFITS

BURDENS

BALANCE

370. Clams Mère Catherine

1. Put 4 dozen clams in a large frying pan over high heat.
2. When they open, add 2 cups heavy cream, and mix with water exuded by the clams. Bring to a boil.
3. Add a bunch of chives roughly chopped. Serve hot.

371. French Shepherd's Pie
(Hachis Parmentier)

1. Peel 2 lbs of potatoes and boil in salted water for 20 minutes.
2. Meanwhile, melt 2 tablespoons of butter in an enameled saucepan. Peel 2 onions and chop in food processor. Put contents in saucepan, cover and cook over low heat for 10 minutes.
3. Add 1 lb of chopped (or ground) leftover steak or roast beef, 1 lb of chopped calf's liver, and ½ bunch of chopped parsley (use food processor).
4. Mash potatoes, incorporating 6 tablespoons of butter and ½ cup of milk .
5. Spread mashed potato over the meat and onion mixture in baking dish.
6. Bake in oven at 350° F for 25–30 minutes. Serve with a green salad.

372. Lamb Brochettes

1. Use 2 lbs of meat from lamb shoulder cut up into 20 1½–inch chunks.
2. Run flat skewers through the lamb chunks. Place a broiler pan beneath the skewered lamb.
3. Broil for 10 minutes, turning lamb over after 5 minutes.
4. Toss the lamb pieces in a mixture of 3 tablespoons Dijon-style mustard, 2 tablespoons of chopped parsley, and 8 oz of bread crumbs.
5. Return to broiler for 5 minutes until crumbs are golden and crusty.

TIME-SAVING TIP INFLUENCE FOCUS

373. Parisian Beef Salad

1. Boil 5 new potatoes in salted water for 20 minutes; let cool.
2. Cook 2 carrots for 10 minutes in simmering beef broth.
3. Cut 1 ½ lbs of roast beef into slices, strips, or cubes, free of gristle and excess fat.
4. Finely chop 1 onion in food processor. Slice 1 pickle into small rounds.
5. Slice cooling potatoes and carrot into ¼-inch rounds.
6. Mix with well-seasoned olive oil and wine vinegar dressing and let sit at room temperature for at least 4–6 hours (meat needs time to absorb dressing).

374. Shrimp en Buisson

1. Cook 1½ lbs shrimp and 1 branch of dill in 8 oz of simmering dry white wine for 3 minutes. Remove shrimp and let cool.
2. Add a good pinch of cayenne pepper and decorate with chopped parley. Serve cold.

375. Spiced Gratin of Crab

1. Cook ¾ lb crabmeat for 5 minutes in simmering contents of 2 cups of clam juice (or 1 ½ cups of dry white wine). Drain.
2. Peel and mince 1 onion in food processor and put contents in a heavy-bottomed saucepan, together with a tablespoon of butter and a bit of salt. Cover and cook over low heat for 7–8 minutes.
3. Add the crab, 1 tablespoon of cognac, ½ teaspoon of curry power, and a pinch of cinnamon. Set aflame, averting your eyes.
4. Add ¼ lb shrimp and a peeled sour green apple cut into small cubes.
5. Wrap 1 teaspoon of thyme, a bunch of parsley stems, and 1 chopped celery stalk in cheesecloth; add it and 2 cups heavy cream to the saucepan and simmer 3–4 minutes; remove the cheesecloth and serve.

BENEFITS

BURDENS

BALANCE

376. Veal Chops à la Crème

1. In a skillet, cook ⅔ lb of mushrooms in a little olive oil over high heat for 3 minutes. Salt and pepper, and keep hot.
2. In the same skillet, add 2 tablespoons butter and, when it sizzles, add chops and cook over medium heat for 4 minutes on each side. Keep hot.
3. Pour ½ cup of dry white wine in the skillet, and boil and scrape up juices and brown bits formed on the bottom of the pan. Add the mushrooms and 1/3 cup heavy cream, and simmer until cream thickens. Pour over veal chops and serve.

377. Veal Cutlets Meunières

1. Melt 4 tablespoons of butter and 3 tablespoon of canola or peanut oil in a large skillet over medium-high heat.
2. When buttery foam begins to subside, introduce 4 lbs veal cutlets and cook for 3 minutes on each side. Keep warm in a heated oven or on plate-warmer.
3. Pour over cutlets juices from cooking, blended with 4 tablespoons of melted butter.
4. Sprinkle with chopped parsley and serve.

SHOPPING

378. Board An erasable board in the kitchen is handy for listing items to get as the thought arises. Household members may pick up some of those items when running errands. The remaining items will be checked off on the shopping list just before the weekly shopping.

379. Bulk Buy bulk quantities and deep freeze perishables you do not plan to use soon. You will need a larger freezer and more storage space, but you will make fewer trips to the store.

 TIME-SAVING TIP INFLUENCE FOCUS

380. Express lanes Before you join a line in the express lane at the supermarket, survey the regular checkout lines to see if you will be served faster there. Cashiers in express checkout lanes that are unoccupied will often process your order even though you have more items than the posted limit.

381. Itinerary Patronize stores that deliver. If you must make several stops for shopping, arrange them in a logical sequence that will save you time. If you are shopping on foot, however, you will want to buy the heavy things toward the end of your errands.

382. List Organize your printed shopping list according to the layout of the supermarket where you shop.

383. Lists Be flexible: follow your shopping list but keep an open mind. You may spot something that will inspire you to prepare a meal you hadn't planned on. You can check other stores if your regular market is out of something on your list—but you will save time if you substitute something else that is available from the same store.

    If you are in search of a specific item that your regular store may not have—say, a nice beef tongue, for example—call ahead and ask. Before you leave the house, locate a store that has what you want. Spare yourself a lot of running around.

384. Lists When you notice you are out or soon to run out of some item, write it down immediately on the pad or board set out for this purpose, or check it on the printed shopping list.

    Glance at the list when you are running an errand to see if you want to pick something up or let it wait for the weekly shopping.

385. Shop by mail You can shop efficiently for some foods by mail. Why not order some of our favorite catalogs and inspect them? Call or use the Web.

    GREATFOOD.COM: 1-800-841-5984 (greatfood.com)
    NEIMAN MARCUS: 1-800-825-8000 (Neimanmarcus.com)

BENEFITS   BURDENS   BALANCE

WILLIAMS SONOMA: 1-800-541-2233 (Williams-sonoma.com)
DEAN & DELUCA: 1-800-221-7714 (Deandeluca.com)
ALLEN BROTHERS: 1-800-957-0111 (Allenbrothers.com)
HARRINGTON'S: 1-802-434-4444 (Harringtonham.com)

There's a huge time saving: Skip travel to the store, parking, searching, waiting for service, packing, paying, carrying purchases, returning home.

It takes time to go through catalogs and you will receive some unnecessary ones. You cannot inspect your purchases beforehand, but most companies have very liberal return policies. Someone must be available to receive the delivery.

You also don't have the "pleasure" of shopping.

386. Shopping List
Use our shopping list below or make your own. One way to do that is to take an inventory in every room of your house: Check the kitchen for groceries, the bathroom for toiletries, the closet for cleaning supplies, etc.

FRUIT/VEG

apricots
apples
asparagus
bananas
blueberries
broccoli
brussel sprouts
cabbage
carrots
cauliflower
celery
chives
cilantro
cider
cucumbers
dill
dried fruit
eggplant
garlic

ginger (fresh)
green beans
green onions
honey
leeks
lemons
lettuce
lemons
lemon juice
limes
melon
mushrooms
nutmeg
nuts
onions
oranges
paprika
parsley
parsnips
pear

TIME-SAVING TIP

INFLUENCE

FOCUS

peas
peppers
potatoes
radishes
raisins
shallots
spinach
squash
strawberries
tempeh
tofu
tomatoes
vanilla extract
zucchini

MEAT/FISH
bacon
beef (lean)
blue fish
chicken breast
chicken roast
cod
cornish hen
crab
duckling
flounder
haddock
halibut
lamb
lobster
mackerel
pork
salmon
scallops
shrimp
swordfish
tuna
turkey
veal

GROCERY
beef stock

canola oil
cereal
chicken stock
clam juice
coffee (decaf)
coffee (reg)
cookies
cornstarch
crackers
deodorant
flour
granola bar
mouthwash
mustard
noodles
olive oil
parsley flakes
pickles
pizza (frozen)
potatoes (can)
rice (white)
rice (brown)
safflower oil
saffron
salad dressing
salmon (canned)
salt
spaghetti
spices
sugar
taco fixing
tea
tomatoes (canned)
tomato sauce
toothpaste
tortilla chips
tuna (canned)
Worcestershire sauce

HOUSEHOLD SUPPLIES
aluminum foil
baggies (large)

BENEFITS

BURDENS

BALANCE

Food 137

baggies (small)
brown bags
bleach
cleaning soap
dishwasher
   detergent
drain cleaner
fabric softener
laundry soap
oven cleaner
paper napkins
paper towels
plastic wrap
polish (metal, furniture)
scouring powder
sponges (abrasive)
stain remover
toilet bowl cleaner
toilet paper
towels (paper)
TV guide
wax paper

DAIRY & BAKERY
bagels
bologna
bread (dark)
bread (white)
butter
butter blend
cheese (cottage)
cheese (deli)
cheese (feta)
cheese (mozzarella)
cheese (nonfat)
cheese (parmesan)
cheese (swiss)
Coke (caffeine free)
Coke (diet)
Coke (diet/free)
Coke (reg)

cream (heavy)
cream (light)
croutons
dessert ice
egg beaters
eggs
ham
herring
ice cream
juice (apple)
juice (cranberry)
juice (orange)
margarine
mayonnaise
milk (1%)
milk (skim)
muffins
orange juice
pasta prepared
sherbet
sour cream
Tofutti
turkey ham
turkey pastrami
turkey sliced
vegetable (frozen)
water
yogurt

ERRANDS
bank
car wash (interior)
car wash (exterior)
cash machine
dry clean
economy
gas station
post office
shoe repair

TIME-SAVING TIP

INFLUENCE

FOCUS

387. Small Stores

Small stores near your home may prove convenient. As a regular customer, you may develop some rapport with the salespeople, who may do you favors like holding a special bargain for you, or calling you when something of interest comes up.

👍 Friendlier atmosphere, less crowded, special favors, better location.

👎 Less choice than in a larger store, sometimes more expensive.

388. Where and When
We advise using the Web to do your grocery shopping if that service is available in your area; in effect, someone shops for you, selecting what you have checked off on your computerized list.

If the Web service is not yet available, consider: Is there someone who (perhaps for a small sum) would shop for you using your list?

If you must go to the supermarket, go at off-hours when the checkout lines are likely to be shorter. Ask the manager when that is—probably weekday mornings. And ask the manager what the opening and closing hours of the store are.

Do not shop when you are hungry; it tends to skew your judgment about what to get.

389. Wine
Order wine in quantity directly from a producer or from your wine merchant. You can do that by phone, mail, or fax. Consider starting a wine cellar if you have the appropriate space. Buying in quantity will save you money and time.

BENEFITS

BURDENS

BALANCE

6

Health and Recreation

HOBBIES

🕐 **390. Community service** Community service can be more demanding of time and commitment than a hobby, but then its rewards are often greater, too.

Consider volunteering for organizations such as the American Red Cross (www.crossnet.org), Human Rights Watch (www.hrw.org), civic groups and church-sponsored activities in your community.

Before you volunteer, research the organization to obtain as much information as you need to determine whether its values and operating style are in tune with your own. Speak with the volunteer coordinator who can help match your skills and expertise to the available volunteer opportunities.

👍 Knowing you are helping out; meeting like-minded people; learning new skills.

👎 Time, some money.

🕐 **391. Down time** All of your time does not have to be accounted for. Not every minute must come under one of the chapter headings in this book, nor reflect your priorities in life.

If you want a little "down time" to just veg out—why not? You deserve it, and you may need it.

392. Gardening
Gardening takes time: Planting, mowing, watering, weeding, spraying, trimming, etc. If you don't mind, fine. If you do, consider hiring someone to help you.

Skilled help that leaves you time to enjoy your garden and spares you the expense of tools and repairs may be worth the extra money.

393. Photo albums
Your photos will mean more to you and your friends, and you will spare yourself time wasted looking for pictures, if you organize them in photo albums and note the event and the date.

Some albums helpfully provide storage for negatives as well. You can buy 3-hole loose-leaf plastic sheets for prints and negatives from Century Photo Products (1-800-767-0777).

Alternatively, devote a wall in your home to photos of family, friends, and loved ones. Stock up on frames when you come across them. To make the framed photos more appealing, buy precut mattes that will fit in standard-size frames and accommodate standard size photographs.

394. Photo mailers
Don't drop off and pick up film and prints at your local photo store. You can save a lot of time by using mailers.

EXAMPLE: Kodak (800-242-2424) sells mailers so you can mail them your rolls of film and they will mail you your slides and prints.

395. Playing the Lottery
If you play the lottery regularly, why not place a weekly or daily order in the store where you buy tickets. That will spare you waiting on line each time you want to play.

BENEFITS

BURDENS

BALANCE

Health and Recreation 141

MEDICAL

🕐 **396. Appointments** Questions for the doctor occur to all of us between medical appointments. If they are not pressing, make a note of them adjacent to the appointment in your calendar.

🕐 **397. Appointments** Yes, your doctor CAN be on time for your appointment if you book early and are forthright about your needs.

- Some medical appointments can be booked long in advance. Do that. Enter the dates for your annual physical and periodic dental visits in your calendar and three months prior to each date enter a reminder to book an appointment. Better yet, book each new appointment at the time of your visit.
- When booking an appointment, explain that it creates a serious problem for you when you are seen late and are therefore late for your appointments. Say: "My day fills up with appointments just like Dr. Gland's does, so I'd really appreciate an appointment when she is most likely to be on time." This may be the first appointment in the morning or after lunch.
- Thank the staff and the doctor when you are seen on time.
- Because the best-laid plans can go astray, bring work with you.

🕐 **398. Condoms** The importance of condoms for sexual relations among people with multiple partners cannot be overstated. Condoms should be placed within easy reach in your bedside table, in a wallet or purse, in a glove compartment, etc.

🕐 **399. Data** Keep a medical record folder for each member of the family and pet in a safe place. The file should contain:

- the dates of shots and surgeries
- a list of medications and vitamins taken
- allergies

TIME-SAVING TIP

INFLUENCE

FOCUS

- names and phone numbers of physicians consulted
- insurance information and cards
- hospital registration cards
- medical data given the patient, such as the results of stress tests, blood studies, etc.

400. Dentist What? You don't love to go to the dentist?

Quarterly visits to your dental hygienist and proper home care between visits with floss and a good toothbrush (replace it regularly) will save you time, money and pain in the long run. Our dentist recommends the Braun Oral-B electric toothbrush.

Dental visits not only insure that your gums stay healthy and that you will keep your teeth longer, they also allow your dentist to check your mouth and detect problems early, while they can be corrected more easily.

401. Family doctor If all members of the family have the same primary care doctor, you will save time. To choose a family doctor:

- ask friends and family for recommendations.
- ask specialists whom you see.
- some hospitals provide physician referral services.
- check the Internet. Some state medical boards report doctors' education and training, awards and publications, disciplinary actions, and paid malpractice claims. The address: http://www.docboard.org.
- Many health plans require you to choose your doctor from their network of health care providers or to pay a supplement when you do not. Ask the plan for their directory of providers and use it in conjunction with the methods listed above, or ask the doctor you have selected with which health plans he or she is associated and choose your plan accordingly.

Your family doctor will know the health history of the entire family in depth; trust will build through the years; the whole family can go for physical exams at the same time.

402. Prescription refills Ask your doctor to give you prescriptions that are renewable and to provide large quantities, so you can minimize trips to the drugstore.

Most insurance plans will allow purchasing three months' of most prescribed medicines.

If you refill your prescriptions every three months, for example, then make quarterly entries in your calendar to remind you to get refills before you run out.

403. Prescriptions Don't go to the pharmacy unless you find some pleasure in it.

- Find a pharmacy that will deliver your prescriptions.
- Use a mail service to fill prescriptions, such as National Rx Services (1-800-950-5070).
- Medicine-On-Time assembles up to 6 medications in a dosage bubble and organizes these on sheets so you take the right medicines at the right time and are spared the tedium of filling pill cases (www.medicineontime.com; 1-800-722-8824).

404. Smoking Consider stopping smoking. You will add years to your life, and spare yourself many illnesses both minor and grave, all time-consuming. You will be seated sooner in restaurants, and spare yourself trips to the store for cigarettes.

- Call the American Cancer Society for a guide on how to stop smoking (1-800-227-2345).
- Make a pact with a friend.
- Sign up for a stop smoking course.
- Use the tools to help you: Nicorette patches to reduce dependency gradually and Wellbutrin (requires a prescription) to reduce craving.

 TIME-SAVING TIP   INFLUENCE   FOCUS

MOVIES & THEATER

405. At home At-home viewing saves time over going to the movie house. You can:

- Rent your movies at the nearest video store.
- Buy their used videotapes, often for less money than two tickets to the movies.
- Spare yourself trips to the video store for rental and return with pay-per-view: Most cable operators provide this service—give them a ring or scan your channels or local newspaper for the pay-per-view program.
- Many cable operators also offer movie channels for a surcharge.
- Join a video club to purchase tapes at sharp reductions (we like Columbia House, 1-800-457-0866).
- Record televised movies with your VCR and watch them at your convenience.

406. Booking Some movie theaters now allow advance reservations by phone. Take advantage of it. To save even more time, dine near the movie house and stop by the theater on the way to dinner. With your tickets in hand, you won't have to wait on line.

407. Booking To find good theater tickets when traveling, try the concierge at your hotel. You may pay a small premium, but he or she will save you time and probably get you better seats than you would have been able to do yourself.

408. Cut-in-line passes Some movie theaters sell passes that allow the holder to go to the head of the line.

409. First night The longest waits (and poorest seating) to see a new movie are opening night and Friday and Saturday nights. Avoid them.

BENEFITS

BURDENS

BALANCE

If you want to go out to the movies on Friday or Saturday night, select a movie that has been out for a while.

 410. Pre-theater dinner Have dinner early THEN go to the theater. You will have better service in the restaurant before peak hours and you will avoid the crowd of people rushing to restaurants after the show.

Many restaurants in the theater district have pre-theater specials or, at least, are familiar with the time constraints of theatergoers. Be sure to tell them you are going to the theater when you make your reservation, arrive at the restaurant, and order from your waiter.

 411. Season's tickets Consider getting season's tickets.

Some performing arts organizations construct subscriptions to insure your attendance at less popular events. Ask them for the date and time when make-your-own subscriptions and individual tickets go on sale for the season. You will have to wait on line that once, but you will have more choice in selecting shows and dates for the season and you may come away with nearly as good seats.

👍 You avoid waiting on line. You can be guaranteed good seats.

👎 You may attend some shows or concerts you would not have chosen otherwise. You must commit to set dates long in advance.

PARTIES

🕐 **412. Attendance** Half of life, they say, is showing up. But you don't have to stay (unless you want to). Choose only the parties you really care to attend. Unless there is a sit-down dinner, arrive a little late—it's a courtesy to your host and will save you time. Likewise, leave when you are ready to go, with thanks to your host and, if necessary, a word of explanation.

TIME-SAVING TIP   INFLUENCE   FOCUS

413. Calendar One way to keep track of social engagements: Get one of those large wall calendars that show a month at a glance, and enter the dates of important parties, birthdays and events you don't want to miss. The whole family can use this calendar with each member entering his or her events.

414. Diets Ask your dinner guests when inviting them if they have dietary restrictions or pronounced food preferences. This can save you time and embarrassment if a vegetarian, for example, announces during dinner that he can only eat the peas and rice— unless you'd be kind enough to prepare some spaghetti.

Some hosts prefer not to inquire as that simplifies food preparation. They reason that it is the guests' responsibility to speak up if they have special needs. A compromise: Dishes of enough variety on the table that most people can skip one and still be satisfied.

Another compromise: Invite people to one meal who you know share dietary proclivities (a fondue party for cheese lovers, homemade sushi for sushi lovers, etc.).

415. Dinner A few large dinner parties make a more economical use of time than several smaller ones. Example: If you and a partner merge two dinner parties for two different couples into one for six people, you gain an entire evening since cooking and cleanup are scarcely greater for six than for four.

Don't have the time to cook for six? Try a catering service; it costs less than you may think; it frees you from shopping, cooking and cleanup, and allows your guests and you to spend time together—which is the point after all.

An intimate dinner party is a special opportunity to spend rewarding time with old friends and to make new ones. Larger parties introduce more people to one another, but they are less likely to deepen your relationships with the guests.

416. Dinner at home Consider choosing a set day of each week or month when friends are usually invited to "potluck" at your home.

BENEFITS

BURDENS

BALANCE

The informality allows you to simplify the food preparation. The regular date makes it easier to invite people since they know when you're likely to entertain and can come at a future date if they can't attend the next scheduled dinner.

👍 Simplifies scheduling; a nice time with friends, a way to keep in touch, a tradition.

👎 The time and additional cost for entertaining—but you can skip some dates.

417. Dinner invitations Use your address book to keep track of WHO came to dinner WHEN and WHAT was served. That will help you recall whom you have (and have not) invited recently and what you served them—lest you feed it to them twice and they think that one dish is your entire culinary repertoire. If they have food preferences, you might note them here, too.

418. Directions Make a sheet with written instructions for driving to your home and include a map and your telephone number. Drive the route after nightfall, note signage carefully and record on the sheet distances shown on your car odometer.

Next give the sheet to someone who is not familiar with the route, ask them to drive it, and have them report on wrong turns, moments of doubt, etc. Finally, revise the sheet and fax or mail it to people who will be visiting you and don't know the route.

When invited to a party, always ask for instructions and the address and phone number and enter these in your calendar or address book. Be sure to take a copy of that information with you.

419. Gifts Keep a supply of cards and gifts on hand for various occasions—birthdays, anniversaries, etc.

Generic good gifts include wine, gift certificates, deluxe soaps, CDs, some books, jigsaw puzzles, etc. When purchasing gifts, have the store gift-wrap them and, if possible, mail them.

Unless you actually enjoy the ordeal of shopping and have time to spare, we advise against entering stores for gifts—it's passé.

 TIME-SAVING TIP INFLUENCE FOCUS

Choose your gifts from catalogs or from the Web (See Communications-Internet).

If you know the brand name of the gift you want, or the name of a store that is likely to sell it, try entering those names in a Web search engine (See Communications-Internet).

Gifts are also advertised in the newspapers along with telephone numbers to place your order (however, if they put you on hold, hang up!).

420. Party check-off list Here is a comprehensive check-off list for dinner parties from small to large:

Decide on date, time, and location.
Plan guest list.
Write out directions to house/duplicate.
Call guests OR
Buy invitations/buy stamps/mail invitations, directions.
Plan menu/consider special dietary needs.
Check recipes for dishes to be prepared ahead of time.
Assess need for caterer/hire caterer.
Assess need for hired help/hire help.
Choose music/hire musicians.
Arrange child care.
Assess space requirements/arrange for adequate space.
Borrow/rent/buy needed furniture: tables, chairs, coat rack.
Count/rent/borrow/buy dishes, cups, serving bowls punch bowl.
Count/rent/borrow/buy glasses and pitchers: wine, liquor water, beer, parfait, punch.
Polish/count/ rent/borrow/buy silverware.
Take out/polish silver: trays, candlesticks, bowls, candy dishes, fruit dish, coffee service.
Take out napkin rings, salt and pepper shakers, sugar bowls, creamers.
Clean tablecloths, napkins, dishtowels, aprons.
Prepare/clean outfit to be worn.
Make shopping list/include the following categories:
    a. hors d'oeuvres
    b. cocktails, drinks
    c. appetizer
    d. entree
    e. vegetables

BENEFITS

BURDENS

BALANCE

f. salad
g. bread
h. condiments
i. nonalcoholic drinks
j. desserts
k. coffee, tea
l. after-dinner candies, liqueurs

Get money to cover expenses.
Buy wine, liquor, beer.
Buy bar condiments and supplies: cherries, olives, onions, lemons, limes, oranges, stirrers, shakers, toothpicks, coconut, pineapple.
Buy mixers, juices.
Buy snack food for bar: peanuts, pretzels, crackers.
Buy paper goods: napkins, bathroom guest towels, coasters, doilies, cocktail napkins.
Buy film, flash.
Shop for food.
Make ice.
Chill wine.
Make list of cooking and cleaning chores.
Prepare foods that can be made early.
Clean house.
Empty dishwasher/clean out dish drain.
Put out guest towels.
Pick up rented equipment.
Rearrange furniture.
Clean out hall closet/put up coat rack.
Prepare space for boots, umbrellas, raincoats.
Check outdoor lighting.
Put out ashtrays, coasters.
Make dinner plans for children.
Buy last-minute perishables.
Buy flowers.
Decorate house.
Make centerpiece.
Load camera/take pictures of table.
Cook.
Arrange seating plan.
Prepare bar/put out ice bucket, tongs, cocktail shakers, condiments, napkins, cocktail stirrers, snack food.

 TIME-SAVING TIP INFLUENCE FOCUS

421. Routine Do you feel that you are "trapped" into some social routines? If so, consider quitting them! It's ridiculous to waste your time—and have a bad time to boot—at events organized for pleasure.

If playing bridge on Wednesdays used to be fun but is no longer, stop doing it. If driving to see your folks at Thanksgiving is an ordeal, how about flying them in to visit you—or meeting for dinner somewhere in between, or visiting a favorite relative, or taking a weekend cruise together? Or begging off until Christmas?

Nothing requires you to attend high school and college reunions, the office Christmas party, weddings other than your own—it's your choice!

422. Service Whether for parties or for dinner, save a lot of steps by using a tray to bring things to and from the table. The best tray has handles, a barrier to prevent things from sliding off, and a surface that can be wiped clean quickly.

Service carts are available that can wheel a substantial amount of food to the dining table. Sideboards with a warmer are also useful for keeping things handy to people seated at the table.

423. Surprise! It's nice to have some drinks and snacks always available in case a friend should drop in unexpectedly. That will spare you an inconvenient trip to the convenience store when you want to be with your guest.

424. Talking politics Most of us, when uninformed about a topic, will say little when it comes up, but for some reason politics is an exception—nearly everyone has an opinion, no matter how ill-prepared to argue it.

Don't waste your time arguing politics with those you meet. You are unlikely to learn much, even less likely to change the other person's views. Yet emotions usually run high and the discussion is hard to curtail.

Other topics will be more pleasant and can save you time—such as advice on movies, child care, shopping, dining, travel and, yes, time-saving tips.

BENEFITS

BURDENS

BALANCE

READING

 425. Bitter end Where is it written that you must finish reading whatever newspaper, magazine or book you bought? If you are not enjoying it, learning from it or, preferably, both, why not set it aside or toss it out? Now you have some time free to spend on your next priority.

426. Bookmark Use your business card as a bookmark. That way, if you ever leave your book somewhere inadvertently, a considerate reader may let you know.

427. Borrowed books It's prudent to write your name in all your books, or to insert bookplates, and to keep a list of books that were borrowed, by whom, and the date.

428. Cancel those subscriptions! If some of your magazines are piling up unread or only skimmed, consider canceling the subscriptions or passing them up at the newsstand. This will save you space, money and time.

If you are receiving catalogs or other unsolicited mail you would like to stop, you can send a note to: DMA Mail Preference Service, PO Box 9008, Farmingdale, NY, 11735-9014. To receive fewer national telemarketing calls, write to DMA Telephone Preference Service, PO Box 9014, Farmingdale, NY, 11735-9014.

429. Information services If you read several newspapers, magazines and the like in order to stay abreast on specific topics, consider subscribing to an information service.

Uncover (email: uncover@carl.org) will search numerous professional journals for you and send you email when articles appear that include your search terms. You can then order them through the service (at a price).

Clipping services can be helpful: check your Yellow Pages or contact Luce Press Clippings, 420 Lexington Avenue, New York, NY, 10170 (1-800-528-8226).

 TIME-SAVING TIP   INFLUENCE   FOCUS

430. Manuals Have you ever seen a manual—whether for computers, VCRs, whatever—that was well written and easy to follow?

Neither have we. Technical writers just don't know how to analyze behavior into its parts; they probably have never tried to follow their own instructions, and if their best language is Japanese that doesn't help.

Sadly, manuals are often the fastest way to the solution of your problem. Contacting tech support or a salesperson can be slow and arduous and there's an excellent chance that person will give you no useful information or even wrong information. Moreover, if you read the manual, you will pick up tips you didn't know to ask about.

Bottom line: Be sure to get the right manual and read it. At least the first time through, read it with the device next to you so you can find the features and try them out. Some manuals are so full of information that you cannot absorb it all in one pass. Read it again. Highlight what strikes you as important.

Reserve a place on your bookshelves for manuals and store them there. It's wise to keep a copy of the purchase invoice with the manual, so when repairs are needed you can answer questions about date of purchase, vendor, and serial and model number.

431. Newspapers Have your newspaper delivered; it saves time.

Buying the newspaper yourself as you take a walk (or walk your dog) is a pleasure. You can also say hello to the newsman. Consider what a city would be like if there were no more newsstands, shops, and the like because most things were delivered or mailed to the home.

432. Organizing books Arrange your books by topic and, within topic, alphabetically by author. When removing a book, lie an adjacent one on its spine, so that you can quickly return the book to its place.

Give away books you are unlikely to refer to (the gift may be tax deductible). Put on upper shelves the books you won't part with but rarely consult.

BENEFITS

BURDENS

BALANCE

433. Photocopying When you photocopy an article from a magazine or book, copy the cover page as well, so that you have the information you need to reference it or to retrieve the original if necessary. Don't keep a magazine or newspaper around because you may want to refer to one or two articles—photocopy them instead.

Using a permanent marker, write the topic (or author's name) and the year of publication in large letters at the top of the first page, staple the sheets, and file the article by topic (or name).

434. Scanning
To scan factual material:

- First look at the table of contents to select what you wish to read.
- Next read the first and last paragraphs of the selection.
- Now read the first sentence of each paragraph, then skip to the next, unless the topic of the paragraph interests you enough to read it in its entirety. This won't qualify you as an expert on the subject, but it will often provide you with the information you need.

435. Solitude "Reading maketh a full man," said Francis Bacon, but where can you find quiet time to read nowadays?

- At the office, you might try a Do-Not-Disturb sign on your door and a Do-Not-Disturb button on your phone. Some busy readers prefer to arrive at the office before the start of the work day, when it is quiet.
- Others prefer to read at home. Can you identify a place that's yours for reading and explain to your family your need for quiet time when there?
- We like to read on planes and trains. It's an example of our time-saving principle of "doubling up," since travel takes time in any event. It signals your neighbor that you don't want to engage in conversation and it makes the trip fly by.
- We also stash light reading (catalogs, bulletins) in a rack next to the toilet.

TIME-SAVING TIP

INFLUENCE

FOCUS

RESTAURANTS

436. Just say no When you call for reservations—and you always should—some restaurants refuse to take them. We make it a point of civic duty to tell them that we will rarely be able to eat there as a result. If we are sorely tempted by a great chef, we may ask on what days and times there is little or no wait for seating, so that we can try it at least once.

Double the waiting time quoted to you by any restaurant host or hostess. Since they are punished for overestimating the wait (prospective clients leave), they generally underestimate it and you are punished instead.

If you often accept long waits to be seated, you must either enjoy hunger pangs while standing in the way of waiters in crowded restaurants or you place little value on your time.

Restaurants that do not honor your confirmed reservations do not deserve your patronage.

If you have a choice, please consider leaving when your seating is delayed more than 15 minutes—the usual limit of the restaurant's patience when you are late to arrive. Increasingly, restaurants, like airlines, are overbooking but unlike airlines, they suffer no penalty for overbooking unless you leave. The common excuse: "Not our fault, those diners are lingering," won't wash: If the restaurant hadn't overbooked the table, it would be vacant.

437. Large parties Since you cannot talk to more than four people at the dinner table, it is rarely worthwhile to have more than four people at the table in a restaurant. When you have five diners, one is often "wing man," looking at an empty chair and remote from the other end of the table, or the group may be spread out around a circular table, making it more difficult to converse. With six diners, people at one end of the table are cut off from those at the other. You may not be able to talk to the fifth and sixth guests but you do have to wait for them to arrive and order, and pay at the end of the meal.

Most of us have attended luncheons to meet candidate X or the newly hired person Y only to find ourselves conversing with a random pick of adjacent diners none of whom is X or Y. Shouldn't we have the courage when invited to say: Sorry, I find those events unproductive. If I really should meet X, I suggest you schedule us to meet.

438. Time constraints No one can match the French in the art of leisurely dining: there can be as many as eight courses, with numerous wines and liqueurs, extending over three hours.

If you are in the U.S., however, and would rather just spend an hour or so, order your meal at the same time you order a drink before dinner. Be firm, say "we are under time constraints this evening so we would like to order the drinks and food at the same time, please." Ask if your selections are reasonably quick to prepare.

The choice of today's specials (or, in France, "le menu") insures a faster dinner as the chef has done some advance preparation, which is not true for many of the regular selections.

Be sure to close your menu and stack the table menus when you have made your choices. An open menu signals the waiter that you are not ready to order.

SEXUAL RELATIONSHIPS

439. Sexual partners Many people, especially singles, spend more time than is necessary in search of sexual partners. Here are some time-wise tips for finding sexual satisfaction, assuming you have ruled out abstinence. Sexual encounters with strangers can be high-risk. You can reduce the risks of HIV and other sexually transmitted diseases by being certain to use a condom.

- Adult literature. Sexually explicit magazines and books can be found in specialized bookstores listed in the yellow pages. A good guide to meeting places such as bars, restaurants, clubs, bath houses, and outdoor cruising spots saves a lot of time.
- Videos. Most video stores carry straight and gay pornographic videos, but some are specialized.

TIME-SAVING TIP

INFLUENCE

FOCUS

- Phone Sex. Many sexually explicit magazines will list telephone numbers for phone sex services.
- Escort services. These are expensive but a great time saver.
- Personals. Place an ad in the personals page of a magazine or newspaper that carries personal ads attractive to you.
- Internet. There are several dating services on the internet. Search for them with a search engine such as Yahoo. (See Communications-Internet).
- Meeting places. Frequent the places that the sort of people you want to meet frequent. These include bars, bathhouses, outdoor cruising spots, gyms. Don't waste time going to the wrong place. If, for example, you want to meet mature men, you are less likely to do so in a discothèque, more likely in a hotel singles bar. Ask the bartender for the best times to frequent the bar; some are popular during the cocktail hour, others fill up late in the evening. One time-wise time to go to bars is near closing time; some patrons are loath to go home alone and will be easier to meet.
- Network. Entertain your friends and they will entertain you and you can meet suitable people at one of their parties. Ask your friends about places to go, and which nights they are most popular. Different bars, for example, are popular with different clientele and on different nights of the week.
- Choose your vacation spots with your interests in mind. Again, friends and guides can help you narrow the field.
- Community activities. Many singles meet one another through community activities such as performing groups, athletic organizations, church-sponsored groups.
- Dating services. There are professional dating services that advertise in the Yellow Pages and on the Internet.
- Candor. You can save a lot of time by being frank. If you feel someone is interested in you and are pleased, don't let the opportunity pass. Risk a little deflated ego and show them you are interested in them.
- Dress. Wear dress that's appropriate to the places you are frequenting and the companions you are seeking.
- Appearance. If you want to meet partners more readily, you must pay attention to your physical appearance and grooming.

Through candor, networking, guides and the other tips given here you can meet partners in much less time.

BENEFITS

BURDENS

BALANCE

It takes time to go in search of a partner and some money, too. There are risks of contracting diseases. Some prostitutes and hustlers may rob you or hurt you. In some areas, this type of socializing is against the law.

Sexual fulfillment is one of life's great pleasures. It is one of the rewards of committed relationships but singles have a right to it, too, and many find life partners in this way.

SLEEP

440. Insomnia

Tips to help you sleep easier:

1. Exercise in late afternoon or early evening.
2. Make sure your bed and room temperature are comfortable.
3. Make the room dark or try using a sleep mask. (Flents: 1-203-847-5390)
4. Make the room quiet or use foam ear stopples. (EAR 1-800-543-8633)
5. Avoid heavy meals, alcohol and caffeine six hours or less before bedtime.
6. Avoid drinking large quantities of fluids close to bedtime that may send you to the toilet during the night.
7. Go to bed and get up at the same time every day, even on weekends.
8. Try stress-reducing moves such as meditation: See Health & Recreation—Stress—Reduction.
9. Unwind and relax by reading, listening to music, or soaking in a bath for a half-hour or so before bedtime.
10. Try to put personal problems on hold until the morning; making a list of them may help.

441. Nap Getting up earlier will lengthen your work day. If you need the sleep, go to bed earlier or take a 30-minute nap in the day (after lunch, before dinner . . .). Experts say it's the equivalent of three hours sleep and may prolong your life. Churchill

TIME-SAVING TIP

INFLUENCE

FOCUS

and Napoleon took naps (separately) and you're no busier than they were surely.

442. Reduction People vary in how much sleep they need in order to feel and perform their best. It is worth experimenting to see if you are sleeping more than you need to. Try reducing your sleep time by 15 minutes a day and see how much awake time you can gain without penalty. Even if it is only 15 minutes, that's 90 hours a year!

"SHAKE OFF THIS DOWNY SLEEP, DEATH'S COUNTERFEIT."
(SHAKESPEARE)

SPIRITUALITY

443. Scheduling Spiritual development is a goal for many people, who find widely different activities fulfilling.

For some it is organized religion; for others, it is the opportunity to experience the grandeur of nature, what Freud called the "oceanic experience." For still others, it is a time of calm reflection and meditation.

If time for spirituality is important to you, let your priorities and scheduling reflect it.

SPORTS

444. Burning calories The goal is to expend 1,000 calories a week. For each of the listed activities, we show the time you would need to engage in it three times a week to achieve the goal.

JOGGING 7 mph — 22 minutes
JUMP ROPE — 26 minutes

BENEFITS

BURDENS

BALANCE

JOGGING 5 ½ mph—27 minutes
RUN IN PLACE—30 minutes
CROSS-COUNTRY SKIING—30 minutes
SWIM 50 yds/min—40 minutes
WALK 4 ½ mph—45 minutes
TENNIS SINGLES—50 minutes
BICYCLING 12 mph—50 minutes
WALKING 3 mph—1 hour
SWIM 25 yds/min—1hour 12 minutes
BICYCLING 6 mph—1 hour 20 minutes
WALK 2 mph—1 hour 20 minutes

 445. Family If you engage in sports like bicycle riding, jogging, golfing or swimming with your spouse or children, you and they will be healthier and you will have a good time together.

 446. Fitness If you think physical activity is for people who aren't smart enough to watch TV, think again. Physical inactivity will cost you time in the long run because it increases the risk of many illnesses and shortens your life. And there are time-smart ways to fit fitness into your life.

Make up a fitness plan that includes aerobic fitness, flexibility, and muscular fitness. You can trade exertion for duration: For example, you can garden or play volleyball for 45 minutes; or walk briskly or dance rapidly for 30 minutes; or run a mile and a half in 15 minutes. The goal is to expend about 1,000 calories/week. Fitness does not have to be expensive. Walking is free, community recreation facilities inexpensive, a gym or aerobics classes cost somewhat more. An aerobics exercise videotape costs $25.

Get a good fitness book to guide you. We like: *American College of Sports Medicine Fitness Book*, available from: ACSM National Center, P.O. Box 1440, Indianapolis, Indiana, 46206-1440 or call Tel.: (317) 637-9200 or fax (317) 634-7817. (Website: http://www.acsm.org/sportsmed/geninfo.htm.) Check with your doctor before starting your program.

Buy aerobic and weight-training equipment for your home. The prices will take your breath away before the equipment does, but it's a time-smart move—if you can afford it. Some recommendations and list prices:

TIME-SAVING TIP

INFLUENCE

FOCUS

- Nordic Track Pro ($600)
- Life Fitness Lifecycle 5500 ($1,000)
- Concept II Indoor Rower C ($725)
- Pace Master Pro Plus H.R. ($1,895)
- Tecktrix Personal Climber ($2,295)
- Tuff Stuff Cardio-Gym ($1,995)

We're told there is more unused physical fitness equipment in the U.S. than Army surplus. You can be sure you will use your equipment if you can afford a trainer who comes to your home regularly. Otherwise, make standing appointments with a friend or trainer at the gym. At home or at the gym, you do need a trainer for progress, efficiency and safety.

You can find a trainer by asking at a health club, or by writing to the ACSM, which certifies them. It is wise to ask if your trainer has a professional diploma, preferably one in exercise physiology.

You will look better, live healthier, live longer.

Fitness requires 1½ to 3 hours per week. Equipment, clothes, club membership and a trainer cost money. Without supervision you risk injury.

447. Fitness Consider running errands or going to work on a bicycle. You need the exercise, you may find that you get there faster, and you will not have a parking problem.

448. Fitness Software FitBody 3.0 is a complete nutrition, fitness, and health tracking system for Apple Macintosh and Microsoft Windows personal computers. When you use FitBody, you can get feedback about your nutritional intake, workout progress, and wellness history. (Website: www.Darwin326.com)

449. Fitness Software Protrack is a software package designed to keep track of your workouts, measurements, and personal fitness goals. Keeping this information on your personal computer allows you to view and analyze your information in graphs and reports. (Website: www.dakotaFit.com)

BENEFITS

BURDENS

BALANCE

450. Preparation Do not risk injury by leaping into vigorous athletic activity without a program of preparation that trains your muscles, reflexes, and circulatory system.

 451. Skiing Unless you ski a lot, consider renting your equipment rather than buying it. You will get in a lot more skiing and enjoy yourself more if you go skiing on weekdays.

Don't neglect the "après ski": Leave the slopes well before they close; most accidents occur in the late afternoon as daylight wanes and so does the energy of the skier.

> You will save storage space at home; you needn't transport your equipment to the ski resort; and you can benefit from the latest improvements in equipment.

> It does take a few minutes to rent the equipment.

 452. Travel Nowadays many hotels have gyms and pool facilities and will gladly direct you to nearby jogging routes.

So buy some lightweight running shoes and swim trunks and take them along on your trips.

Remember to tell your travel agent that you prefer hotels with athletic facilities.

 453. TV Do you find exercise boring? If so, put a television set within view. Tape some of your favorite programs, so you will have something to watch that is to your taste.

You can also purchase used movie tapes from your videotape store, or inexpensive tapes from a mail order house.

With your eyes glued to the box, the minutes using your Nordic Track or other equipment will seem to fly by.

TIME-SAVING TIP

INFLUENCE

FOCUS

STRESS

454. Detection
A stress self-diagnosis checklist.

- Are you tired, irritable, and sleeping poorly?
- Do you have headaches, neck or backaches?
- Do you have dry mouth, excessive sweating, reduced appetite?
- Are you "medicating" stress with alcohol or nicotine?

Avoid time wasting sub-optimal performance; avoid health crises.

Taking a moment to check in with yourself; the unpleasant reminder that you are human and your body imposes limitations on what you can accomplish.

455. Reduction Excess stress makes you less productive, less well, and less agreeable to be with. Ways to reduce stress:

- Take a coffee break (preferably decaf).
- Stand up and stretch.
- Call a friend.
- Take a catnap.
- Use the tips in this book to free up extra time.
- Keep to your fitness program.
- Follow the advice of a good stress-reduction book, such as *Principles and Practice of Stress Management* by Paul Lehrer and Robert Woolfolk.
- Follow the advice of Harvard researcher and physician, Dr. Herbert Benson: "Evoke the relaxation response for 10 minutes daily. Sit quietly and focus on your breathing. On each out breath, repeat a short phrase; disregard other thoughts that come to mind."

Two strategies for stress reduction often overlooked are working harder and its opposite, letting go. Many students "'stressed out" at the approach of a final exam, for example, reduce stress by studying long hours, and are relieved to find that they are increasingly prepared.

BENEFITS   BURDENS   BALANCE

Once you have done what you can do, if you can let it go, you will accomplish more in other areas and suffer less stress. This is especially true if you find yourself trying to control the behavior of a family member—child, spouse, parent, etc. Are you trying to manage more than is within your power? Are you teaching them how to depend on you, thus increasing your time commitment and stress?

456. Reduction Try making a worry list.

Put down on paper all your primary concerns about the week ahead: doctor's appointment, sales meeting, visit from an ex-spouse, whatever. Writing them down may defuse those concerns a little.

Next to each concern, write down your worst fears: cancer; I'll fall asleep; we'll fight. That may defuse them a little more.

Review the list at the end of the week. Were your worries justified?

Admittedly, if your worries are so straightforward, you haven't mastered the art of worrying, which consists in letting everyone know you are worrying (they will show concern), while hiding, even from yourself, what's disturbing you, deflecting it onto specific weekly worries instead. When the specific worries clearly do not materialize, you will surely find other worries to clothe your angst.

457. Reduction When you get home and before you start any chores at home, do this to reduce stress:

- Change to more comfortable clothes (consider "sweats").
- Sit down, take off your shoes, and put your feet up for a moment.
- Take a deep breath and stretch.
- Have a cup of tea or a cold beverage.

458. Vacations Here is how to make a nice stress-reducing vacation into sheer hell:

1. Promise yourself to finish every undone task in your life before leaving on vacation.
2. Book an exhausting trip to a very remote place and keep changing hotels once you are there.

TIME-SAVING TIP

INFLUENCE

FOCUS

3. Choose places where you will suffer from jet lag and return to work before you can get acclimated to the time zone.
4. Haul an absurd amount of stuff with you, including lots of work. Don't forget your cellular phone.
5. Tell everyone in your professional and private life how to reach you on vacation.
6. Travel with young children.
7. Leave young children behind.
8. Visit all the sights in your six guidebooks.

SUPPLIES

459. Pill containers Buy some convenient plastic cases for pills, with compartments labeled by days of the week. You can buy them at any large drugstore.

A pill case will help you keep track of whether you remembered to take your medication. And it saves time to fill the case once a week rather than select pills from their several bottles each day.

> "ONE PILL MAKES YOU TALLER /AND ONE PILL MAKES YOU SMALL /AND THE ONES THAT MOTHER GIVES YOU /DON'T DO ANYTHING AT ALL."
>
> (GRACE SLICK)

460. Spare eyeglasses If you need prescription eyeglasses, buy at least two pairs, so you are not stranded when one is lost or broken.

If you use eyeglasses primarily for reading, buy inexpensive magnifying glasses at your drugstore and put spares in your glove compartment and office, by your bed and telephone, and wherever else the need arises repeatedly.

BENEFITS

BURDENS

BALANCE

WALKING

🕐 **461. Aerobics** Oh, happy the manual laborer who digs ditches all day—he needs no fitness regimen. But if the only thing you dig is computers and you do not have time to exercise 30 minutes three times a week as we recommend, consider these (relatively) painless moves:

- Take a walk after dinner.
- Take the stairs instead of the escalator or elevator.
- Park at a little distance from your destination. Often it takes less time to walk to and from a nearby destination than to get the car, drive through traffic, park, retrieve the car, drive back, and park again.
- Walk on some errands. Walking is often faster than public transport, too. Riding a bicycle around town is another excellent aerobic activity that may actually save time—but beware of time-urgent drivers who have read this book!

> "I NAUSEATE WALKING; 'TIS A COUNTRY DIVERSION,
> I LOATHE THE COUNTRY."
> (WILLIAM CONGREVE)

🕐 **462. Breaks** Take a healthy break such as walking rather than just a coffee break.

Stand up and stretch. Take a walk around the block or run an errand.

If you want to work as you stroll, carry a voice memo recorder with you so you can put your thoughts on some topic in order and jot them down orally. (Communication-Techniques-Memo recorders.)

TIME-SAVING TIP

INFLUENCE

FOCUS

Home

BASEMENT/ATTIC

463. Central heating Relying on fuel deliveries can cost ⏱ you some time and trouble.

Consider getting gas heat or, somewhat more expensive, electric heat.

464. Lights Can't see in the dark? Your hardware store sells a ⏱ simple system that switches a light on when you open the door and shuts it off when you close it.

👍 You need not look for the light switch, nor free up a hand to operate it, nor remember to turn it off.

👎 Buying and installing the unit.

465. Organization There's a force that makes unwanted ⏱ things spin off toward the attic or the basement. Be courageous: discard or give away things you never use (Goodwill Industries, the Salvation Army).

For treasured items, take a moment to label their cartons or bags for faster retrieval.

BATHROOM

 466. Bath If you love to take long baths, why not "double up" and do some of your reading while you're there — as President Kennedy did.

You can also listen to the radio, watch TV, or play language tapes (but respect safety rules with electrical equipment).

Immersible pillows and backrests for the bath are available.

 467. Medicine cabinet Throw away medications that have passed their expiration date, old empty prescription bottles, and toiletries of one sort or another that you never use.

 468. On the throne Louis XIV delivered speeches from the toilet seat; a famous lord claimed he learnt all Latin poets while there.

Many people read a newspaper, catalog, or magazine in that locale. You may find that you can "double up" and do serious reading there.

 469. Shower Showers are generally faster to take than baths.

Some people "double up" and shave in the shower.

A wall-mounted dispenser for shampoo, conditioner, and soap also saves a little time and contributes to safety.

 470. Supplies Buy supplies in bulk for common toiletries (soap, toilet paper, toothpaste, mouthwash, razor blades, Qtips, etc.); keep one week's worth in reserve in a bathroom cabinet.

When you draw from the reserve, put those items on your shopping list.

 TIME-SAVING TIP   INFLUENCE FOCUS

471. Time savers

To keep your teeth and lose your beard:

- An electric toothbrush cleans more effectively for the time spent brushing.
- An electric wet/dry razor won't nick you when you're in a hurry and, used with shaving cream, it shaves almost as close as a blade.
- A fog-free magnifier mirror will help you shave or apply makeup accurately.

BEDROOM

472. Bed sheets
For faster bed-making, use fitted sheets for bottom sheets and comforters rather than top sheets and blankets.

473. Linen
In order to see right away which sheets are king, queen, twin etc., choose a different color for each type.

CLEANING

474. Blinds
VERTICAL blinds, made of vinyl, that slide along a track are preferable to HORIZONTAL Venetian blinds.

They are easier to operate; they catch much less dust and, if a slat breaks, you can replace it without replacing the entire blind.

475. Broken glass
For swift and safe cleanup of broken glass, use a damp paper towel. You will get all the pieces without cutting your hands.

BENEFITS

BURDENS

BALANCE

⏲ 476. Dust

"TIME HATH AN ART TO MAKE DUST OF ALL THINGS."
(THOMAS BROWNE)

Carry a bucket or basket that has your primary cleaning tools and solutions. Work systematically. Example, cleaning a house: start at the top of the last flight of stairs and move clockwise from room to room, then floor to floor. Within each room dust from high to low.

Clean surfaces with furniture, glass or general-purpose cleaner. Repeat the circuit with a vacuum cleaner, cleaning furniture, drapes and rugs or carpets as necessary. Check the filters for air-conditioning and heating at the start of cooling and heating seasons.

⏲ 477. Garage sale Resist junk takeover!

Annually, go through your house from attic to basement and set aside all the clothes, books, gadgets, furniture, etc. that you haven't been using.

Invite friends to select from the lot, hold a yard or stoop sale, or deliver items to charity.

⎈ 478. Hiring a housekeeper A great housekeeper

becomes a man (or gal) Friday—an invaluable asset. You may recover the money a housekeeper costs you if you turn your time freed up to profit. Or you may find the time for one of your neglected priorities.

Ask friends to recommend someone. Some housekeepers are inner-directed and know instinctively how to keep your house the way you want it to be, others are outer-directed and need a list of tasks to accomplish each day.

Give the housekeeper some autonomy and you will be glad you did. Ask him to buy things that he notices are running out, to mend things that need mending. Caution: Last-minute requests may prevent the housekeeper from doing some of the household chores.

Authorize the housekeeper's signature at the hardware store and grocery store. Agree on enough hours to get the job done. Pay enough so the housekeeper likes the job, will be creative, and stay with you.

TIME-SAVING TIP

INFLUENCE

𝒫

FOCUS

479. Schedule It's best to clean your house on a schedule—certain days for certain tasks. That allows you and others in the household to plan around those events.

> **EXAMPLE:** If you know the day on which dry cleaning is normally dropped off and picked up, you know what will be in your wardrobe.

480. Tools

FOCUS ON TOOLS FOR CLEANING
Broom
Brushes
Bucket
Dust cloth
Duster
Dustpan
Floor polisher
Mop
Paper towels
Rags
Rubber gloves
Rug shampooer
Sponge mop
Sponges (abrasive)
Spray bottles
Stepladder
Tool-carrier
Vacuum cleaner

CLOTHING

481. Alterations When you buy new clothing at a store that is not near your home, you will save time by having the alterations done at a tailor shop that is near you. This is all the more true if the original alterations need to be adjusted.

BENEFITS

BURDENS

BALANCE

482. Bow-tie Formal wear requires a bow tie and you may like to wear them on other occasions, but they are the very devil to tie properly. Fortunately, there are quite good ones you can buy that are pre-tied.

There's something classy about knowing how to tie your own bow-tie. Or have your significant other do it as you press little kisses to her forehead.

483. Buy double When you buy a shirt or slacks, consider buying two.

When the first pair is at the cleaners, you can wear the second.

You spare yourself the time to go out and shop for that pair on a separate occasion, also save on the time it takes to try things on for fit.

484. Buy off-season Who would buy swim trunks in the winter and overcoats in the summer? You, if you're time-wise.

Buy off-season and you can take advantage of better prices and smaller crowds.

485. Children Most parents have their children clean up and dress for school *before* breakfast, so that they can leave for school right after breakfast.

However, if your children wash and dress *after* breakfast, they can brush their teeth after the meal and they don't risk getting food on their school clothes.

486. Closets Dual-level closets conserve space, since a tier of shirts or blouses placed over a tier of slacks or dresses puts all clothing within easy reach. Pants keep their creases longer if they are hung from pants hangers. Garment bags protect clothing from dust and moths.

A shoe rack can be positioned at the bottom of the closet although that makes the shoes awkward to reach. If you have spare hanging space, there are shoe bags with Velcro fasteners that tie around the hanging bars. There are also shoe bags that

TIME-SAVING TIP

INFLUENCE

FOCUS

mount on the closet door. (Get the catalog from Hold Everything: 1-800-421-2264, or visit their website at www.holdeverything.com.)

Coats and longer items will require a standard single-bar clothes closet.

487. Closets For the children's closet, an adjustable twist bar is handy: You can move it up as the children grow and their skirts or pants get longer.

488. Closets To dress more efficiently, arrange your hanging clothes in four groups: slacks, shirts and blouses, two-piece outfits, and dresses. Within each group, arrange the clothes from light to dark.

No need to scan your entire collection of ties, belts, and shoes each morning if you keep them arranged by color.

489. Disposal Give or throw away clothes you rarely wear (you don't like them any more, they don't fit anymore, styles have changed . . .). Don't keep them for dirty jobs: Other cast-offs will take their place.

490. Dressing Put a comb and pen and pencil in every jacket, put a handkerchief in every pair of pants, leave belts in pants.

491. Dressing Yikes, I'm late!

Do you dress in a panic in the morning, for fear of being late to work or school?

Would five minutes make all the difference? Why not put out tonight all the clothes you will wear tomorrow morning? If you already do that, how about shaving five minutes off your sleep time—you won't miss them.

492. Easy maintenance
Keep it simple:

- Buy clothes that can be washed and don't have to be ironed.

BENEFITS   BURDENS   BALANCE

- Pick fabrics that are wrinkle resistant.
- The fewer buttons the better, as they will not need to be replaced.
- Favor fabrics on which minor stains or spills do not show.
- Favor clothes with a rather loose fit: They are more comfortable to wear, and the seams are less likely to rip. And in the sad eventuality that you add a little, as the French say, embonpoint, they will still fit.
- Athletic gear made from high-tech fabrics (wicking polyester, etc.) are essential for workouts and especially useful on trips, as they can be washed, hung dry, and reworn frequently.

493. French cuffs

French cuffs may be elegant but threading cufflinks through them with your left hand and retrieving those that fall under the dresser takes time. They are best reserved for formal attire.

494. Grooming

Choose a hair style that is easy to maintain. Ask your hair stylist or barber at what times they are least busy, most likely to honor your reservation, and to attend to you exclusively until you are done.

Book a string of regular appointments at those off-times, so you will not have to call to make each appointment.

495. Grooming

Makeup is not camouflage: It is just meant to underline your natural beauty and to minimize minor defects. Keep it simple. You will save time every morning and throughout the day.

496. Marking children's clothing

Identify each child's clothes with an indelible marking pen or iron-on personalized labels. This will allow you and the children to sort and find their clothes faster.

497. Quality

Buy quality. The extra expense will prove worth it as you can wear those clothes longer, look nicer, and spend less time shopping in the long run.

TIME-SAVING TIP   INFLUENCE   FOCUS

498. Repairs When you buy a suit or shirt, you may get a piece of the material and spare buttons. If so, place them in an envelope labeled to identify the item of clothing, and store the envelope in or near your sewing kit.

499. Shoes Loafers are faster to get into and out of than tie-ups; no laces to replace, either.

500. Shopping When possible, shop for clothes using catalogs or the Internet. If you do go into the stores, go on off-hours and days (call and ask when those are). If you prefer, go with a friend or family member, but not one who is shopping!

501. Shopping When shopping for an item that matches another (a tie with a shirt, a blouse with a skirt, etc.), wear that other item or carry it with you.

502. Shopping When shopping for clothes that require trying them on, wear clothes and shoes that are easy to take off and put back on—no buttons, no laces, as few layers as possible.

503. Size Consider frequenting some of the finer stores that keep a record of your sizes and styles so that when you go there they can provide you promptly with clothes that will fit and are likely to please.

If you can find a clothing store that is mostly in tune with your own taste (and budget), you will save a lot of time by starting there first when purchasing clothes.

If you are satisfied with the selections, prices, and returns policies available from catalogs or websites, by all means spare yourself the trips.

504. Wallet Most men keep too much stuff in their wallets, encumbering themselves, spoiling the line of their clothes, and making them root through debris repeatedly.

All that most men need to carry in their wallets are a credit/ATM card, a driver's license, a check, some money and possibly a business card. Women can also pare down the contents of their purses.

505. Watches A watch with a legible date is handy. An alarm is also useful to remind you of appointments, or to provide a convenient excuse for ending a conversation.

Since it is inconvenient when your watch battery dies, you may want to have it changed annually, say when Daylight Savings Time goes into effect.

ENTERTAINMENT

506. Equipment

FOCUS ON EQUIPMENT FOR HOME ENTERTAINMENT:
TV
VCR
Fast rewinder
Ceiling mount screen
Projector, Carousel
Local refrigerator
Videotape organizer
Tray Organizer (for Carousel)
Universal TV Control (instead of one for TV, one for VCR)
Hi-Fi (with remote control)
CD player (with remote)
CD organizer

507. Photography For your next camera purchase, consider buying a digital camera, instead of one that requires film. (Example: Nikon Coolpix 1-800-526-4566; nikonusa.com.)

You don't have to buy film, nor have it developed, you can see at once what the picture looks like, and you can create a slide show using your TV or computer screen.

TIME-SAVING TIP

INFLUENCE

FOCUS

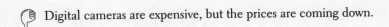 Digital cameras are expensive, but the prices are coming down.

508. Tapes Keep one virgin blank tape near the VCR in case you want to record something unexpectedly.

509. Television Many intelligent consumers are utterly baffled by the proper use of their VCR and TV and waste significant time programming them.

- When possible, buy the VCR and TV together from the same manufacturer; they can be interconnected so that, for example, when the VCR is playing a tape, the TV/VCR switch automatically selects VCR.
- Modern VCRs come with automatic time setting (the time signal is buried in the TV signal), programming by code numbers (that are published in the newspaper or magazine TV schedules), and program display on the TV screen.
- In the store, try changing channels using the TV only, then try that using only the VCR. Now program the VCR to record your favorite show. If you find these maneuvers complicated, don't buy the equipment! Some recommended equipment:

Toshiba M782 (list $600): 1-800 587 9316; Toshiba.com
Panasonic PV-4662 (list $380): Panasonic.com

510. Television You can save considerable time and some pain by watching TV shows that you have recorded with your VCR rather than live. When watching the taped program, fast-forward through the advertisements and any segments that don't interest you. Some VCRs do this for you, automatically.

You can program your VCR to tape programs that you watch regularly, whether daily or weekly. You need only program it once, and you'll always be able to view your programs at a time convenient for you.

To help you limit the time you spend watching TV, place the device out of the way if you can, rather than in the living room.

BENEFITS

BURDENS

BALANCE

FAMILY

511. Babies Calming a crying young child (ages 2–5) can be a challenge. We found that positioning the child in front of the TV while playing a cartoon videotape often does the job.

With crying infants, once you have exhausted the obvious remedies (food, burping, diaper change, rocking) try turning on a fairly loud sound source such as a vacuum cleaner.

512. Baby equipment Suitable equipment can help you save time in caring for your baby and contribute to safety.

> Portable crib (EvenFlo Happy Camper Bassinet 344811; List $100)
> Nursery Monitor (Gerry Range Check Nursery Monitor 610; List $35)
> Car seat (Century Smart-Fit 4525; List $55)
> Stroller (Gracco full-size stroller 7775; List $146)
> Check out Babyfurniture.com on the Web or by phone: 1-877-302-2229.

513. Bulletin board Buy a message board so that all members of the family can post messages for one another. Erasable marker boards are handy and cost about $30 from office supply stores (for example, Highsmith, 1-800-558-2110); cork-boards and tacks work nicely, too.

514. Child behavior Americans are notorious world-wide for raising ungovernable children. Of course, not all of us do, but poorly disciplined children are a burden to their families and themselves.

1. The first step in governing their behavior is to acknowledge that you have great power to dole out rewards and punishments and to provide models, and therefore great responsibility to do so wisely. You are always sending your children a message, explicit or implied, about appropriate behavior—

TIME-SAVING TIP

INFLUENCE

FOCUS

even if the message is your passivity, understood as "do as you like."

2. The practice that promises the most refractory children is the one Americans engage in most—inconstancy. Inappropriate behavior that sometimes brings its rewards and other times not—demanding to be the center of attention, for example—is the hardest to ever extinguish. Make reasonable rules, so that you can stick by them, and then do so. Take stock of the rewards and punishments at your command and mete them out contingent on the child's actions.

3. Behavior is controlled not only by its consequences but also by its antecedents, its settings. What is appropriate in one time or place is not in another and we all had to learn those distinctions when growing up. If you spend time working at home or engaged in personal study or reflection, your children must come to recognize the inviolability of that time. You can help them do that by choosing clearly demarcated times and places for your work and never rewarding their intrusions into those times and places.

As the children get older, consider setting up a token economy. Tokens are convenient to dispense, agreeable to hoard, and flexible in value—they are much like the adult practice of clipping coupons. You can decide, or negotiate with your children, on the token cost of various rewards (five gets you to the movies) and the token reward of various actions (raking the lawn gets you five). As a rule of thumb, the least attractive activities should earn the largest number of tokens.

515. Children

To encourage your children to do their chores:

- Make a list or chart of tasks for each child; for example: Lucy, Tuesdays, set table.
- Be specific: Instead of "clean your room" try "put your toys in the toy basket," "put your shoes in the shoe rack," etc.
- Set up a token economy with colored poker chips. State the chip value of completing each task correctly and on time. Promptly reward completion. Chips can be traded at intervals for privileges, treats and/or money.

BENEFITS

BURDENS

BALANCE

516. Children Even young children can prepare their own breakfast if you buy individual size servings of cereals and milk.

517. Children To encourage young children to keep their space tidy, put up pictures of things over the spot where they should be stored: a photo (or sketch) of shoes next to the shoe rack, toys next to the toy box, etc.

518. Delegate You can save time by delegating chores at home to family members (or an employee). Change the following list to meet your needs and distribute those chores at a family meeting. Children and pets can be useful and should be invited. The least attractive chores should come with greater incentives, such as money, less time spent on other chores, and services from other family members.

One way to assign tasks: Divide the house into areas that need about the same amount of work—kitchen, bedrooms and baths, outdoor areas, etc. Each family member takes responsibility for an area—indefinitely or on a rotation. Then list specific tasks by area.

CHORES AT HOME THAT YOU CAN DELEGATE (AND SUGGESTED MINIMUM AGE OF THE COLLABORATOR)

Baby-sitting (teens)
Baby-sitting, arranging for (adults)
Bathrooms cleaned (10)
Beds made (8)
Car to repair shop (teens)
Chase mice (cat 1)
Child care (teens)
Children taken to activities (adults)
Clothing shopping (adults)
Cooking with supervision (8)
Destroy unwanted furniture (cat 1)
Dishes in dishwasher (8)
Dishwasher unloading (8)
Fetch newspaper (dog 1)
Food shopping (teenagers)
Food shopping supervised (10)
Home office (adults)
Homework assistance (teens)

TIME-SAVING TIP

INFLUENCE

FOCUS

Ironing (10)
Laundry, put away (5)
Laundry, loads (10)
Lawn and garden (10)
Meal planning (adults)
Pet care (10)
Pickup around the house (10)
Planning social events (adults)
Plants watered (8)
Repairs in house (teens)
School activities and PTA (adults)
Table clearing (8)
Table setting (5)
Toys put away (5)
Vacuuming (10)
Wastebaskets emptied (10)

 Your time is freed up; sharing chores can be a pleasant time of family interaction, in which children learn important skills and all family members feel they are collaborating.

 You may need to teach, monitor, and reward performance. It may cost you money.

519. Family time
Reserve time to spend with your family.

Mealtimes are a frequent choice for sharing ideas, concerns and pleasures.

Openness is part of a family's quality of life, but incidentally it does save time when family members feel comfortable expressing their concerns.

Stay home with your family on Saturday nights and at other peak times and enjoy family life. Save restaurants, movies and the like for times when other people are less likely to go.

520. Getting to work
Does the day start stressfully in your household, with everyone trying to bathe, dress, wolf down breakfast, gather books and papers, and rush out the door at the same time? To make things go more smoothly:

BENEFITS   **BURDENS**   **BALANCE**

- Time it so that some family members (usually adults) get up and dressed before the others and get breakfast started.
- The night before, set out preparations for breakfast and let everyone prepare their clothes and papers for the morning.
- Give every family member a role in common tasks such as preparing and cleaning up after breakfast.
- Retire and wake early enough to have a good night's sleep yet leave time for the morning's chores.
- Prepare a fallback plan for unexpected events: What will you do if the car won't start or if Mom has an early meeting?

521. Gifts Oh, the anguish of finding the right gift! It's enough to forswear all birthdays including Christmas. If you are squandering your money, don't also squander your time.

Consider giving gift certificates. The gift of a dinner at a fine restaurant; a night at a festive hotel. A contribution to your friend's favorite charity.

Children will appreciate a budget they can spend on themselves. In this way you also give them the gift of exercising their own taste and respecting their own priorities.

The pleasure of giving a friend or loved one exactly the right gift is matchless; it is worth whatever time is required.

522. Good-byes Accustom your children early to leave-taking. After a hug and a kiss and a "bye now," you go. Don't let your child learn that by making a fuss he or she can delay your departure.

523. Pooling Baby-sitter pools, school-travel pools, and day care pools are great ways to save on your time if you are a parent.

Frees up your time, some of the time.

You must provide some of the shared services and monitor their quality and reliability.

 TIME-SAVING TIP INFLUENCE FOCUS

524. Quiet time Set aside some time each day for quiet time and explain your plan to your children. Example: After dinner, you get an hour off in which, normally, you are not to be disturbed. On occasion, you may want to feed the children first, then use the quiet time to dine with your spouse.

525. Telephone Young children love to answer the phone. Put a pencil holder and a pad of pre-printed forms next to the phone and show children how to use them to record who called and their message. Mind you, pad and pencil by the phone are handy for adults as well.

FURNISHING

526. Catalogue ordering Stay put and buy almost anything using catalogues or the Internet—from clothes to gadgets, from food to furniture.

- Ordering by phone: call during off-hours, pay by credit card.
- Ordering by preprinted form: This may be faster. Have a stamp made up with your credit card number and expiration date.
- Ordering on the Internet: See Communications-Internet.

527. Clutter
Focus on good things to throw away or give away:

- Baby clothes and toys the children have outgrown
- Books you have read that you are unlikely to use again
- Boxes things came in that are long gone
- Broken appliances
- Canned goods you're unlikely to open
- Clothing that isn't you and you just don't wear
- Clothing you hate to admit will never fit you again
- Duplicates such as corkscrews
- Excess chopsticks and packets of soy sauce

BENEFITS

BURDENS

BALANCE

- Excess gift boxes
- Excess shopping bags
- Exercise equipment that you haven't used in years
- Gadgets you never use
- Luggage you never use
- Moth-eaten items
- Old cosmetics
- Old half-finished projects
- Old luggage you never use
- Old personal papers and magazines you are unlikely to consult again
- Old prints, wallpaper and carpeting you are unlikely to use again
- Old toiletries, medicines
- Shoes and other clothes that don't fit
- Silly souvenirs
- Spices you never use
- Unidentified keys
- Worn out and mismatched socks
- Worn out underwear

 528. Filing cabinet If you run a household, you manage a small business.

You have an inventory, you buy and sell, you own insurance, file tax returns, etc.

So of course you need file cabinets.

Buy one or more from the catalog of any office supply store (e.g., Staples: 1-800-333-3199), along with Pendaflex hanging folders and insert labels.

It may take you a little while to set up your filing system, but you will save time and have a better chance of finding things as a result.

 529. Flood
If you have had a flood:

- Dry the surfaces to avoid mildew.
- Wash clothes, professionally clean furnishings.
- Clean and dry all household appliances before using; don't use washing machine or dishwasher unless the water is safe and the sewer line works.

TIME-SAVING TIP

INFLUENCE

FOCUS

- Put liquid bleach in toilet bowls.
- Discard porous items that could be contaminated.
- Rinse and freeze valuable papers & photos until restored.
- Rinse computer tapes and disks, insert in a plastic bag in the refrigerator.
- Discard porous toys.

530. Mirrors A mirror in the hallway, by the door, lets you check your appearance on the way out. It also makes the room seem larger and brighter.

531. Shopping
Shopping for furnishings?

- Draw up a list.
- Check Consumer Reports Buying Guide for brand ratings, price, features to look for. You can search it online for a small membership fee. (www.consumerreports.org)
- Keep an eye out for relevant advertisements and catalogs.
- Call manufacturer, supply house or department store to place an order or
- Order by catalog or
- Search the Internet, order there.
- Do not shop in the stores. It takes too much time. You may need to go to more than one.
- You can (almost) always return something you ordered if, once delivered you conclude it isn't what you wanted.

532. Sofabed Some sofabeds are easy to open but many have a supporting iron bar that seeks out your shoulder blades during the night. Get one with a thick mattress and try it out for comfort. When your friends (or your children's friends) are visiting overnight, you will be glad you did.

533. Stain prevention Most fabrics and clothing will be stain proof (or, at least, retarding) if you spray Scotch guard fabric protection (available at your hardware store).

BENEFITS   BURDENS   BALANCE

534. Storage Write the contents of a storage carton in large letters on the carton—you'll find things faster.

If that's not fast enough, number the cartons and make a list of what is in each. Then mount the list on the wall or put it in your computer.

535. Upkeep Do you love polishing copper, brass, and silver? We didn't think so. Choose ceramic or glass instead.

In general, bear upkeep in mind when buying furnishings.

Copper bowls, silverware, trays, and candlesticks are beautiful and worth the time to polish.

KITCHEN

536. Appliances & utensils The winner in the most ingenious device category is the Screwpull. It removes corks from wine bottles with astonishing ease; you will never want to use any other corkscrew once you have tried it. Source: Le Creuset of America (1-803-589-6211).

For recorking bottles, especially champagne bottles, it's best to buy bottle caps at your hardware store.

Now, here's a handy checklist for the well-furnished kitchen:

APPLIANCES
Blender
Brisker
Coffee maker with clock
Compactor
Dishwasher (Recommended: Sears Kenmore 19525; List $600)
Dispose-all
Electric beater
Electric can opener
Electric Crock-pot
Electric kettle
Electric knife

TIME-SAVING TIP

INFLUENCE

FOCUS

Electric knife sharpener
Electric juice squeezer
Electric rice-cooker
Electric waffle maker
Food processor
Freezer (Side-by-side Refrigerator Amana SRD 2555
    List $1749)
Jar opener
Microwave (rotating + dual function) (Sharp R 9H66
    List $550)
Paper towel dispenser
Plate warmer
Range, Gas (G.E. JGBP24BEW List $599)
Refrigerator with ice dispenser (see freezer)
Scale
Self clean oven
Timer
Toaster or toaster oven

UTENSILS
Apple corer
Basting brush
Colander
Corn holders
Cutting board
Escargot holders
Garlic press
Grater
Grinder
Knife set
Lobster and nut crackers
Potato peeler
Rolling pin
Salad dryer
Scissors
Sifter
Skimmer
Spatula
Steamer
Tongs
Whisk
Wooden spoons

BENEFITS

BURDENS

BALANCE

Pots and pans
Bread pans
Casserole dishes
Cookie sheets
Cooler
Double boiler
Dutch Oven
Muffin pan
Pressure cooker
Pyrex ware
Roasting pan with rack
Skillet, 10 in with lid
Tupperware
Wok

537. Clutter Inspect your kitchen drawers and shelves.

Isn't it time to say goodbye to useless glasses—former mustard and jelly jars, beer and shot glasses? Goodbye to chipped and dented pans and cracked plates never used. Goodbye to three-of-a-kind utensils.

Now you have some space for time-saving tools you really need. For example, a pressure cooker.

538. Coffeemaker

Buy a coffeemaker that

- is electric
- has two brewers; one will serve for regular coffee, the second for decaffeinated coffee or a supplementary supply of coffee
- allows pouring before the end of brewing (but be sure it's easy to insert and remove the carafe)
- has a programmable clock, so that your coffee is ready for you when you come into the kitchen in the morning
- keeps the coffee hot on a hot plate but shuts off automatically before it burns the coffee
- a gold filter basket so you won't have to mess with paper filters and risk running out of them

Want the ultimate coffeemaker at any price?
With the push of a button, in just 50 seconds the Capresso

TIME-SAVING TIP

INFLUENCE

FOCUS

Coffee and Espresso Center grinds, tamps, brews and cleans and delivers a cup of coffee brewed from regular to strong, your choice. There's also a frother that makes toppings for cappuccinos or lattés and a hot water dispenser for instant hot tea. The Claris Water Care System removes any chlorine, lead, aluminum and copper for better taste. (About $900 from www.cooking.com.)

539. Cooking
Don't be one of those insouciant chefs who makes repeated trips to the convenience store at the last minute.

Read the recipe all the way through as you make a list of needed ingredients. Plan ahead, so that purchasing them can be part of your weekly food order. When it's time to begin, lay out all of the utensils you will need to prepare the meal.

Stack the dishwasher with soiled dishes and implements as you proceed, then run it at least an hour before dinner so that it can be emptied before the meal and will be ready to receive the dinner dishes. Place pots and pans that are emptied at serving time in the sink, run some water into them, and let them soak during the meal. Scrape and, if necessary, rinse dinner dishes and place them in the dishwasher as they come off the table. Many dishwashers have pre-rinse, rendering your rinsing unnecessary—try it.

540. Cooking double
Don't hesitate to cook more than needed—even cook double the needed quantity: it's no more work, and leftovers can be frozen or saved in the refrigerator. Many dishes even taste better on reheating, as the flavors of ingredients meld into each other with time.

541. Cupboards
Just as the photographer puts shorter people in the front row of a group photo, you should place cans and boxes in your cupboard according to their height. Or try arranging items alphabetically, especially containers that look alike such as spices.

Keep like items together in the refrigerator and in refrigerator drawers.

BENEFITS

BURDENS

BALANCE

542. Drawer Dividers Use drawer dividers to organize your silverware, utensils, and boxes of baggies, aluminum foil, etc.

543. Ice cubes The best solution to the need for ice cubes is a refrigerator that delivers them, but the device takes up a lot of usable freezer space.

Ice cube trays are not easy to use.

Special plastic bags that you fill with water to make ice cubes have recently come on the market. Ask at your hardware store.

544. Organization Are your spices near the stove, are your dishes and silverware near the dishwasher? In general, do you keep things near where they are used?

545. Oven cleaning Cleaning an oven can be a long and unpleasant task. It's best to have a self-cleaning oven, but even they have to be cleaned. To make quick work of it, line the oven with aluminum foil and enclose food during cooking, thus avoiding spatter on the oven walls and door.

546. Pans Scrubbing pans is no fun: Get non-stick pans—for example, those coated with Teflon. They are generally a good choice, although occasionally a recipe may call for a standard pan, as those for omelets sometimes do.

547. Plastic wares For some parties, plastic-coated paper plates and plastic cups and utensils are perfectly appropriate and will save you considerable time.

Reserve that type of things for outdoor parties. The pleasure and elegance of dining with fine china, glassware, and silverware is worth the effort of putting them through the dishwasher.

 TIME-SAVING TIP   INFLUENCE   FOCUS

548. Recipes Put all the recipes you clip out from magazines in albums like photo albums. A loose-leaf binder system is best so that you can maintain the set of recipes in alphabetical order.

549. Slicing & peeling

- Meat slices faster and easier if it's partially frozen.
- You can peel garlic cloves faster if you mash them lightly with the side of the blade of a chef's knife.

550. Spices

Two ways to organize your spices for fast retrieval:

- Arrange spices alphabetically on the shelf.
- Put the most-frequently used spices in one place, the rest in another. If you have the space, a plastic "lazy Susan" is helpful, as a spin of the wheel lets you scan your spice collection.

551. Storage Number your plastic storage containers with a permanent waterproof marker such as Marks-A-Lot. Assign the same number to each container and its top, so that it will be quicker work to find proper pairs.

552. Storage Plastic snaps are quick and easy for resealing plastic bags, metal twist-ties are a nuisance (and can clog your disposal or dishwasher). (Lechters: www.lechters.com)

553. Storage

To keep more things ready to hand:

- Slide-out shelves
- Telescoping pull-out tables
- Rotating trays
- Hooks on the wall, backs of doors, in corners for pans, towels, aprons
- Storage racks above head for glasses

BENEFITS

BURDENS BALANCE

- Storage on the tops of cabinets and other hard-to-reach places for infrequently used light items (reach with a stool or stepladder)

554. Storage When the food storage bags and containers you use are transparent, you can see more readily what you have stored in your refrigerator.

555. Storage Wire-mesh storage baskets, open shelving and wall-mounted racks are often less expensive than enclosed kitchen cabinetry and allow you to find and replace kitchen items more rapidly.

LAUNDRY

556. Claim checks If you pick up your own laundry, dry-cleaning, or shoe repairs, carry the stub with you in your wallet or purse so that it is handy if some errand places you near the cleaners.

Many cleaners accept shoe repair requests, sparing you an extra trip, and some even deliver to the home.

557. Ironing To avoid ironing, remove clothes from the dryer as soon as possible and fold or hang them.

When possible, select clothes that do not need ironing.

558. Socks For socks in everyday use, two solid colors will probably suffice: black and brown. This makes sorting and pairing socks easier and faster. And when a single sock gets lost or worn out, you need not throw the pair away.

559. Sorting You will make quicker work of cleaning clothes if they are pre-sorted. Buy laundry baskets of different

TIME-SAVING TIP   INFLUENCE   FOCUS

colors, one for hot wash, one for more delicate fabrics, and one for clothes to go to the cleaner.

560. Washer-dryers We advise against buying combined washer-dryers, unless you really need the saving in space. With two separate machines, you can do another load of wash while the first one is drying.

LIVING ROOM

561. Ashtrays Buy ashtrays with a lid that hides cigarette butts and extinguishes any that remain smoking. You need empty them less often.

562. Books and tapes You could number books, tapes, CDs, etc. with permanent adhesive labels (Avery 1-800-462-8379), then make a table that shows the contents assigned to each number.

Finally, place the items in numerical order.

If you prefer to do without a numbering system, you can arrange these items topically—for example, all the folk CDs in one place, opera in another, etc. Then, order them alphabetically by author, composer, or performer, within topical group.

563. Extra bed If you have a couch you use occasionally as a bed, put a set of sheets and a pillow case in a plastic pouch and slide it under the couch for easy bed making when necessary.

564. Fireplace If you buy firewood, buy your wood in spring or summer: you will save time and money and have drier wood to burn.

BENEFITS BURDENS BALANCE

⏱ 565. Appliances

- Check Consumer Reports first when choosing appliances. Prefer the brands that have fewer repairs.
- Buy major brands from major stores; you are likely to need fewer repairs and to obtain them more readily.
- Some maintenance contracts include preventative maintenance. It's a good idea: A broken appliance is likely to remain broken for a couple of weeks—the time it takes to schedule a repairman to diagnose the problem, get new parts, and replace the defective parts.

⏱ 566. Bulbs
Keep a backup supply of all the types of light bulbs you use. If some are difficult to reach, buy long-life bulbs from your hardware store or electric company.

567. Delegating
Are you all thumbs or do you simply dislike doing repairs? If so, you could ask another member of your household to do them or to help.

Failing that, keep a list of the repairs you need. Ask among your friends for a "handyman"—someone who is good at doing minor carpentry, electrical repairs, plumbing, painting, etc.—and give the handyman the list of problems to resolve. When the list is long enough and the repairs major enough, you can successfully call a general contractor or individual technicians. However, these professionals feel extremely unloved and it usually takes many calls and much cajoling to get them to your home to give you an estimate, to start the job and—most difficult of all because they like to overlap jobs—to complete the work.

If at all possible, add a clause to your agreements that rewards the vendors if the work is completed on time or punishes them if it is not.

⏱ 568. Deliveries
Increasingly, American households are unoccupied during the day but delivery services and tradesmen persist in requiring you to be there when it is economical for them to arrive. Some ways to cope:

- Have deliveries made to your office, your neighbor, or a nearby business such as Mailboxes Etc.

 TIME-SAVING TIP   INFLUENCE   FOCUS

- Avoid having items delivered that you can conveniently pick up or have picked up.
- Book appointments with tradesmen in the evenings or on weekends when possible.
- Hire someone to stay home and wait for them.
- Ask for a telephone number you can call on the day of the appointment to fix the projected time of their arrival more exactly.
- Ask among your friends for a handyman who will be more flexible in scheduling than a business.

569. Fuse box Have all your fuses or circuit breakers clearly labeled. There is a card for this purpose on the door of the fuse box, or you can make one up. To label a fuse with the room, devices, or outlets it controls, find an accomplice who will tell you which lights or devices go on and off as you flip the circuit breaker (or unscrew the fuse). Shut down computers before you do this.

Note the amperage of your fuses and keep some spares with the needed amperages in or near the box.

570. Heating and cooling Verify that your air conditioners are working properly in late spring (put a reminder in your calendar).

Clean the filters at that time.

Check your heating system in the fall. Some winter heating contracts include an annual preventive maintenance visit to insure that the equipment is working safely and efficiently; sign up.

These measures will spare you uncomfortable waiting in the busy season.

571. Lists Post on each of your major appliances (washer, dryer, hot water heater, central heating, etc.) the number to call when it breaks down. Put those numbers on an emergencies list next to the phone, along with the numbers to call for auto claims, doctors, electrician, plumber, etc.

BENEFITS

BURDENS

BALANCE

572. Paint When the façade or interior of your house is painted, make careful note of the paint brand, color name and code, interior or exterior, and type of finish (glossy, flat, etc.). Keep that information in your home repairs file for the day when touch-up or repainting is required.

573. Stains Keep a stain removal guide in a handy place, so you can administer the proper first aid. For example, carbonated water and paper towels are a good way to treat spilled red wine.

The United States Department of Agriculture distributes a great stain-removal guide (1-202-512-1800).

574. Storage Store things that go into your utility closet such as extension cords, light bulbs, hooks and adhesives, etc. in clear plastic boxes and label the boxes before storing them.

575. Tool list It is a great time saver to do your own simple home repairs, or to delegate them to family members or versatile household help. To get the job done well and efficiently, you need a tool chest on hand with the proper tools. Review this list for possible acquisitions.

Chisel
C-clamp
Cutting pliers
Drain unclogger
Electric drill
Extension cords
File
Fuses
Glues
Hack saw
Hammer
Johnny pump
Mineral spirits
Nails
Nuts & bolts
Oil, household
Outlet adapter

 TIME-SAVING TIP   INFLUENCE   FOCUS

Paint brushes
Paint remover
Pencil
Plane
Pliers
Razor blades
Sanding disks
Scraper
Screwdrivers
Screws
Snake, plumber's
Solder
Soldering gun
Tape measure
Tape, duct
Tape, electrical
Tape, masking
Utility knife
Washers
Wire Stripper
Wood saw
Wrench, Allen
Wrench, plumbers'

576. Vacuum system
In a multi-level home, a central vacuum system spares lugging equipment from floor to floor, although it can be costly to purchase and install.

577. Water heaters
Replace your hot water heater before the end of its useful life, some seven to ten years. If you wait beyond that time you will experience one of the more unusual design features of this appliance: When the insulating glass is fatigued, it cracks, flooding the room where the hot water heater is located and damaging rooms directly below.

BENEFITS

BURDENS

BALANCE

MOVING

578. Checklist According to the U.S. Postal Service, the average person moves about 12 times during his or her lifetime.

"The Mover's Guide" tells you how to get organized and includes a checklist of some of the things to do when you move. It is available at no cost from any U.S. Post Office (call them). It reviews what to do one month, two weeks, one week, and the day before you move, and also tells you things to do when you settle in your new home after the move. "The Mover's Guide" advises you on packing up and unpacking and on how to stay connected (phone, cable, services, and utilities) and the guide includes a change of address card to make sure your mail is forwarded to you.

You may also find this information on the Internet at: www.usps.gov/moversnet. For cable transfer, call 1-800-NU-CABLE (1-800-682-2253). Many moving expenses are tax deductible: Save all receipts and call the IRS for details at 1-800-829-3676.

OFFICE

579. Automatic payments Convert as many monthly payments as possible to automatic payments deducted from your checking account. This will spare you processing bills such as telephone, electricity and gas, water, mortgage, etc. You can verify the direct deduction amounts when you reconcile your checking statement and make entries at that time for tax deductible expenses.

580. Banking Try to do your banking by phone, on the Web, and by mail. Get cash at ATMs. Ask your bank to assign a banker to you; then you have someone to call who knows you when you want to request by phone a funds transfer, foreign draft,

 TIME-SAVING TIP   INFLUENCE FOCUS

or other operation that might normally require you to go to the bank.

If your bank requires you to go there for certain services, ask for a supervisor and present your problem: You never go to institutions such as banks, but you would like to remain their customer. If the supervisor doesn't have a solution, consider changing banks (and let the bank know about it); also consider changing branches; sometimes a smaller or bigger branch provides quite different service from the others.

If you absolutely, definitely, positively must go to the bank and there is no alternative, at least avoid peak hours.

581. Bill paying Use Checkfree (1-800-882-5280) or a similar service in conjunction with bill-paying software such as Intuit's Quicken (1-800-446-8848).

It's faster than writing a check, entering it in a ledger for tax purposes, placing the check in an envelope, stamping it, and mailing it. Moreover, you can program the check to be issued on any date, thereby keeping funds in your checking account longer.

For the occasional checks you need to write yourself, print them on laser-printer checks using the software and mail, if need be, in double-window envelopes.

582. Bill paying If you do not use software for bill paying, you might want to use a tickler file. Toss each incoming bill into your to-pay box, first verifying that it can wait to be paid until your semi-monthly check-writing session. In that session, write checks for all the bills that should be paid in the next two weeks, insert in envelopes and stamp them. Finally, place those payment envelopes in a tickler file according to the date when they should be mailed.

(For instructions on how to set up a tickler file, see Home-Office-Tickler file.)

583. Bill paying When you write out a check to pay a bill, note on the bill before filing it the date, amount paid, and check number; if you later receive an unpaid bill notice, you can track the payment more easily.

BENEFITS   BURDENS   BALANCE

584. Briefcase Don't use your briefcase for filing. Put in it just what you need to carry that day, and empty it at the end of the day.

585. Business cards To store the business cards that are given to you, purchase a 3-ring binder, a set of alphabetical section dividers, and plastic insert sheets for holding business cards (Century Photo Products, 1-800-767-0777). If you add some sheets of 3-hole paper, you can also jot down merchant references given you by friends under their generic headings, such as carpenter, electrician, etc.

Have your own business cards printed with tasteful design and stock; they are a facet of your image. Put on them your name, phone and fax telephone numbers, email and postal addresses. You may want to put your title and affiliation as well. (Business Book, 1-800-558-0220.)

586. Coins Carrying too many coins can be a nuisance. We put the day's collection in cups labeled for pennies, nickels, dimes and quarters. We replenish the coin purse in the car with these coins, for tolls and parking. They're useful for photocopying and laundry, too. You can turn coins in for bills at the bank, if you are willing to roll them up in papers provided by the bank. You can buy a machine to roll for you for $30. (Sharper Image 1-800-344-4444.)

587. Directory Make it a habit to enter telephone numbers and addresses you are likely to need in your address book, Rolodex, or computerized contacts manager.

588. Disaster When disaster strikes, it is often compounded by serious problems of time management and stress. To reduce your risk and time loss, change the following list of disasters to fit your situation. Then, consider what you can do to prevent each disaster and to save time if it occurs.

PROPERTY
- Robbery. To review: insurance coverage; security measures; inventory list; proof of purchase; picture file of possessions;

 TIME-SAVING TIP   INFLUENCE   FOCUS

access to policy numbers and phone numbers for police, insurance agent, claims adjuster, locksmith, credit card issuers; social security number engraved on appliances; credit card numbers recorded; home office coverage; computer coverage; computer backup tapes stored elsewhere.

- Fire. To review: insurance coverage; access to phone numbers for fire department, insurance agent, claims adjuster; fire extinguishers (recommended: Kiddie FA 340hd); smoke detectors (First Alert 10-yr. Lithium); fire-proof safe deposit box or safe; fire hazards; flashlights; candles; fire escapes; fire ladders; first aid kit.
- Flood. To review: insurance coverage; condition of roof; documents off floor in basement; electrical boxes high off floor.
- Car theft. To review: insurance, including auto rental provision; anti-theft devices; Consumer Reports lists of frequently stolen vehicles; garaging.
- Car accident. To review: insurance; accident wallet in glove compartment; cellular phone in car; first aid kit; flares; phone numbers for insurance, hospital, police, lawyer, car rental, garage.

HEALTH

- Serious illness. To review: posted phone number of cardiologist or doctor; emergency medical team, ambulance; review medical insurance coverage; disability coverage; long-term nursing insurance.
- Mugging. To review: exterior lighting; routes to and from house and work; self-defense devices.

EMPLOYMENT

- Loss of supplemental income. To review: savings; salary; cash flow; equity in home; training or investment opportunities; professional contacts; your resume; home office possibilities.
- Loss of job. To review: insurance; savings; home equity; spousal income; professional contacts; your resume; home office possibilities.
- Object of a suit. To review: liability insurance; legal contacts; protection of assets.

BENEFITS

BURDENS

BALANCE

- Death of a relative. To review: funeral arrangements and cemetery plot; estate planning; joint ownership; will; power of attorney; "living will"; organ donation; access to safe deposit box.

👍 Less chance of disaster, and preparedness when it does strike.

👎 Time in drawing up the list and setting up preventative measures; cost in risk reduction, such as insurance.

🕐 **589. Disposal** Don't keep or file what you won't use again.

🕐 **590. Equipment** Nowadays, there's frequent need to photocopy documents. If you do not have a pharmacy or other store around the corner with a photocopy machine for public use consider buying a "personal copier"; Staples (1-800-333-3199) sells several brands.

A combined printer, copier, fax machine may meet several of your needs for little more cost (but you cannot copy pages from books with such a device). If you have a computer, another possibility is to buy a scanner, which will allow you to convert documents to machine processable form, but also to photocopy them, in conjunction with your computer printer. (See Computers-Hardware-Advantages.)

🔍 **591. Filing**

A HOME FILING CHECKLIST: Papers you may want to file:
Adoption papers
Appliance manuals and warranties
Birth certificates
Bonds and stock certificates
Business correspondence
Car license and car tax data
Children's folders (papers about camp, school, etc.)
Citizenship papers
Contracts
Copies of wills

TIME-SAVING TIP

INFLUENCE

FOCUS

Credit card information
Current bank statements
Current canceled checks
Death certificates
Deeds
Divorce decrees
Donation records
Employment records
Entertainment information
Family health records
Health benefit information
Health records
Household improvements
Household inventory
Income tax working papers
Insurance policies
Inventory of safe-deposit box
Investments
Loan statements and payment books
Log of car service and repairs
Marriage certificate
Medical: paid-bills
Memberships, licenses requiring yearly renewal
Mileage
Paid-bill receipts
Paycheck stubs
Personal correspondence
Prescription drugs, dental, eye care, etc.
Real estate taxes
Receipt for safe-deposit box
Receipts of items under warranty
Resume
Titles to automobiles
Travel information
Veteran's papers

592. Filing

Creating or reorganizing your home or business office filing system.

1. Make a list of all your folders, preferably on a computer with word processing software.

BENEFITS

BURDENS

BALANCE

2. Identify the inactive files and remove them to a storage area. Cardboard boxes for holding files are available from your office supply store.

3. Identify the broad categories into which the active folders fall; these will be the labels of your file drawers. Reorganize the list so that related folders come under their appropriate file drawer labels. Alphabetize the list by file drawers or impose some other organizing principle (e.g., dates).

4. Next to each folder name on your list, indicate whether it is a major theme or a subhead. Major themes will get hanging folders, subheads, manila insert folders.

5. For each of the major theme folders, indicate whether the quantity will require an ordinary hanging folder or a one-inch box bottom folder or a two-inch box bottom folder.

6. Purchase the required number of standard hanging folders, 1- and 2-inch box bottom folders, and third-cut interior manila folders. Also buy: three-inch plastic tabs that insert in hanging folders; Avery Index Maker-3 sheets of cardboard inserts for the tabs; sheets of labels for the manila folders, for example Avery 6266. (Choose the type of inserts and labels for a laser printer or a dot matrix printer depending on which one you have.)

7. In order to use your word processing software to print the cardboard inserts and labels, set the tabs and margins as instructed by the instruction sheets that come in the insert and label packages. If you use MS Word, select Tools-Labels-Options and select the corresponding Avery number. Then select New Document, and a template will appear on the document page. (Templates are also available on diskette for just the cost of shipping and handling from Avery.)

8. Copy the master file of label headings and segregate them into folder labels in one file and subhead labels in another. In each case choose the font and size of letters that appeal to you, bearing in mind that the labels are 3 inches wide.

9. Start with the file of manila folder labels, the subheads. Select as many subheads as there are labels in a single column of the label sheet, cut, change to the window in which the template appears, and paste. Repeat for column two. Test print the template page using ordinary paper. Adjust the page setup margins as necessary. Print the sheet

TIME-SAVING TIP

INFLUENCE

FOCUS

of labels, then generate a new template sheet, copy the two columns of subheads onto it, and print, proceeding in this way until all labels have been printed. Repeat for folder inserts.

10. Apply the labels to the first set of interior manila folders that will go in the first file folder. Position the label high on the tab, and select left-, center-, and right-tab folders in succession. Depending on the volume of papers placed in the manila folder, crease it along one of the folding lines at the bottom so the contents sit flat in the folder.

11. Place the set of manila folders in a hanging file of appropriate width, attach the plastic tab at the far left, and insert its cardboard label.

12. Proceed to the next set of subheads.

13. Prepare labels for the drawers.

Save time on filing and retrieving documents.

Takes time and a little money.

593. Filing Avoid using paper clips: they tend to fall off or to catch on other papers. Staples are better and an electrical stapler is a very handy device.

594. Filing When you have purchased new furniture, appliances or software for your home, make a photocopy of the paid bill and file it with the instruction manual in the home purchases file.

As a filing principle, use either the brand name or the store where you bought it, or make two copies and file them under both headings for ease of retrieval. The original goes into the yearly alphabetical file of bills you save.

You may want to know the cost of something you bought years earlier, or to check if the warranty period has expired. By keeping an up-to-date home purchases file, you will not have to search through several annual files looking for the original bills.

Making a photocopy; additional filing.

BENEFITS   BURDENS   BALANCE

595. Filing space If you are short of filing space and don't want to buy more file cabinets, consider using expandable file pockets, accordion files, and shelf files with label holders. Then place these items on shelves (Highsmith 1-800-558-2110).

596. Funeral Although few of us like to linger over thoughts of our death, it is prudent to decide now how you want to be buried and to take necessary measures such as buying a grave or cremation niche, and establishing a funeral trust with a reputable funeral home. Discuss these decisions with others who care for you and encourage them to do likewise.

597. Installation When setting up a home office bear in mind the need for electrical outlets and outlet strips to serve numerous devices such as computer, printer, postage meter, photocopier, lamps, sharpener, telephone, letter opener, stapler, calculator, answering machine, fax, mobile phone recharger, TV, stereo.

Adequate lighting is essential and see our tip on the ergonomic workstation (Computers-workstation).

598. Lists for guests If you entrust your home to friends or tenants while you are away, be sure to give them a copy of your emergencies list (see Home-Maintenance-List) as well as a description of where things are to be found in your home, shops and services in the neighborhood, and your itinerary with instructions for contacting you.

599. Location Your choice of where to locate your home office—when you have a choice—is important as it will influence your working capacity.

Do you prefer to have a desk by a window or will that distract you? Do you want to be alone or would you prefer to be near people? Do you prefer to work in the morning or in the afternoon—when will the sun come into your office? If possible choose a space that has a door and that you will use solely for an office (avoid bedrooms).

TIME-SAVING TIP   INFLUENCE   FOCUS

600. Personal correspondence Keep a box of note ○
cards or personal stationery at hand. You will find them useful
when you want to send a word of thanks, attach a note to a gift,
or send a friend a letter.

601. Postage Don't stamp each letter or bill as you put it ○
in an envelope; do all your franking at once at the end.

Never (well, hardly ever) go to the post office. How can you
avoid it? See Communications-Mail-Stamps.

602. Power of attorney Consider giving power of ○
attorney to one or two very trustworthy persons who need to act
on your behalf from time to time. "Power of attorney" enables
them to conduct business for you, to sign documents and checks
in your place, to gain access to confidential information. Your
lawyer will draw up the document, or standard forms can be
found at your public library.

603. Rubber stamps Purchase rubber stamps or stick- ○
on labels for frequent repetitive inscriptions such as your name
and address, your signature and account number for check
endorsement, first-class mail, air mail, etc. Most office supply
stores will prepare stamps and labels, or contact Business Book
(1-800-558-0220).

604. Scheduling One way to find quiet time for home ○
office work is to rise earlier than others in the family; another is
to retire later. Consider sliding your period of sleep back or forward in the day.

605. Software Software we recommend for your home ○
office (also see our tips under Computers):

Backup Software: Seagate
Check paying service: Checkfree
Data transfer: LapLink
Database: Microsoft Excel

BENEFITS   BURDENS   BALANCE

Email: Microsoft Outlook; Eudora
Fax software: Symantec Winfax
Internet: Microsoft Internet Explorer
Money management: Intuit Quicken
Records management: Microsoft Access
Schedule + Contacts: Microsoft Outlook
Taxes: Kiplinger Tax cut
Utilities for safety and improved computer performance:
    Norton Utilities
Voice-mail: Symantec Winfax Talkworks
Word Processor: Microsoft Word

606. Standing Are you—like Albert Camus and Ernest Hemingway—one of those people who thinks faster standing up? If so, there are standup desks available: Levinger (1-800-544-0880).

607. Supplies

FOCUS ON HOME OFFICE DEVICES AND SUPPLIES:

Address book and/or Rolodex
Book stand
Book weight
Bulletin board, or several squares of stick-on cork
Business cards
Calculator
Calendar/planner
Carbon paper
Clipboard
Computer disks and storage containers
Computer paper and supplies
Copier paper and supplies
Desk clock
Desk lamp
Dictaphone
Dictionary, and other references—airline guide, etc.
Electric stapler
Erasers
File folder labels
File folders.
File rack for desktop files

 TIME-SAVING TIP INFLUENCE FOCUS

Hanging files (Pendaflex)
Highlighters
In box and out box
Index cards
Letter opener
Mailing labels
Mailing/package tape
Manila envelopes and Jiffy bags
Marking pens
Pads, various sizes
Paper clips, regular size and oversized
Pencil sharpener
Pencils and pens
Postage meter
Postage scale
Post-it notes
Rubber bands
Ruler
Scissors
Scotch tape and dispenser
Scratch paper
Stamps
Staple remover
Stapler, staples
Stationery and envelopes
Telephone extension
Thermos
Three hole punch
Typewriter and supplies
Typing paper
Wastebasket

608. Supplies Buy duplicate supplies of ballpoint and marker pens, scissors, staplers, stapler removers, Post-it notes, scotch tape and the like, and keep them at the various locations where you frequently need them. ○

609. Tax return How is completing a tax return like filling a doctor's prescription? Both are purposely unintelligible to the layman so that they remain the work of specialists. ○

BENEFITS

BURDENS

BALANCE

Even though you may use software to keep track throughout the year of your taxable deductions and software to prepare your return, it's unlikely you can do a better job than an accountant because the rules are so complex.

Save yourself some time, some anxiety, and possibly some money by giving the task to a reputable accountant early in the new year (the cost is tax deductible).

⏱ 610. Telephone

To be put on hold less often:

- As soon as the other party answers, say "Please don't put me on hold. I'm calling because . . . "
- If you are put on hold, hang up. If enough of us did that, businesses would stop the practice.
- Buy a telephone with an incorporated speakerphone; when they put you on hold, put them on speakerphone and turn your attention to another task. Be sure to mention that you don't appreciate being put on hold when your party comes back on the line.

⏱ 611. Tickler file
A "tickler file" is a way of organizing paperwork such as bills to pay and letters to answer so that they are completed quickly and on time.

- Number thirty-one folders with days 1 to 31 and label twelve folders with the names of the months, starting with the present month. (Smead Inc. 1-651-437-4111 makes such a combination file but you can use hanging folders.)
- Place all of the materials that need to be processed in the current month in the appropriate day folders and all those to be processed in future months in the corresponding months folders.
- Each day, process the contents of that day's folder. When the first day of the following month arrives, distribute the contents of that month's folder into the day folders and repeat the cycle.

⏱ 612. Waiting for a reply
If you send someone a letter and are waiting for a reply, drop a copy of that letter in your tickler file, or make an entry in your calendar, under a later date.

TIME-SAVING TIP

INFLUENCE

FOCUS

When that date arrives, your copy will remind you to prompt your correspondent for a reply, if you have not already received one.

ORGANIZATION

613. Co-housing Co-housing is characterized by private dwellings with their own kitchen, living-dining room etc., but also common facilities such as lounges, meeting rooms, recreation facilities, library, workshops, childcare. (www.cohousing.org)

Also check out cooperative living by contacting the National Cooperative Business Association (www.ncba.org).

614. Going out Position a shelf, table or credenza close to the door with a bowl or basket for keys, outgoing mail, wallet, cell phone, laundry receipt, theater tickets, coupons, etc. You will be more likely to remember them on your way out.

615. Grouping Whether in the kitchen, the bedroom, the office, or the garage, place things together that are used together and as close as possible to the point of use.

Example: sheets, blankets, pillows go together in or near the bedroom; towels, bathrobes, and the soap supply go together in or near the bathroom.

616. On the fly When you pass an open drawer, close it; a full ashtray, empty it; some loose papers, put them in the to-file box.

If you keep things organized in the course of other activities, you will find you need fewer blocks of time to tidy up.

617. Saving steps If you have stairs in your home, position tables, shelves or credenzas near the stairs on each floor and place on that surface the things that need to change floors, such as outgoing mail, items to be stored or used on another floor, etc.

BENEFITS   BURDENS   BALANCE

There are straw baskets with two levels that are designed to sit on the stairs.

PETS

🕐 **618. Care** Many devices are available from your pet store that make it easier and faster to take care of pets:

- Automatic food and water dispensers
- Self-cleaning litter pan
- Electronic collars, which allow your cat or dog to open a special door when it wants to enter or leave the house
- Electronic devices that administer a mild shock to animals that stray beyond a perimeter (defined by an underground cable)

🕐 **619. Feeding** The pleasure of pretending that pets are like people is a major reason we have pets but if you overdo it, it will cost you time.

Give your pets dry food (veterinarians say it is better for gums and teeth and better balanced than leftovers). If your pet doesn't overeat, leave a supply of food, and of course water, available all the time—that way the pet won't interfere with you when it is hungry.

🕐 **620. Ownership** Consider the pro and cons before getting a pet. Pets are enjoyable—great company for kids, and they can be an occasion for teaching children responsibility. They also brighten the lives of elderly people, especially those living alone. And some dogs make good guard dogs.

But what an investment of time! Walking the dog, for example, buying food, feeding, cleaning up hair, repairing furniture, cleaning the cat's litter box, trips to the vet, arranging care for your pets when you are away. And a pet can do serious damage. Sir Isaac Newton's dog, Diamond, knocked over a candle and set fire to his master's papers and home.

TIME-SAVING TIP   INFLUENCE   FOCUS

SECURITY

621. Children Have your children memorize such important numbers as 911 and where they can reach you or friendly neighbors. You can also program these numbers in your phone's memory so that the children just have to press a single button.

622. Door intercom Consider having an interphone system that allows you to open your front door remotely, once you have identified the caller. Most manufacturers of home and office telephone systems, such as Lucent Technology (1-800-247-7000), have door-phone units for sale that operate using your telephones.

It is more polite and pleasant to open the door and welcome your guests in person.

623. Fire drills What will you and your family do if a fire breaks out in your home? Call 911. What else? Review the escape routes and practice them. Where are your fire extinguishers?

624. Flooding Floods are more common in some states and regions than others. If you live where a flood may occur, be prepared with flood insurance, emergency phone numbers, an escape plan, and the minimum tools for fast cleaning (see Furnishing-Flood).

625. Garage door If you park your car in your garage, a remote control for opening and closing the garage door will save you steps and time.

626. Keys Consider buying a key rack to hold all your house keys, each labeled with the door it unlocks—garage, back door, front door, etc. Also, give a spare front door key to a neighbor.

BENEFITS   BURDENS   BALANCE

627. Keys If you have many keys on a key ring, some probably look alike and can delay your finding the right key for a given lock. You can adopt a color code by buying colored caps for the keys from a locksmith or by painting them with nail polish.

👍 Fast key selection.

628. Proof of loss If fire or theft strikes your home, photographs or a movie showing your possessions will be a great asset in dealing with your insurance company. Store the photos or film in a safe place. You may also ask your insurance company to validate the pictures before you store them.

629. Valuable papers Valuable papers such as birth and marriage certificates, social security, military, and divorce papers, which you rarely refer to but want right away when you need them, should all be secured in one safe place. You can buy a fire resistant safe for your home, or put the papers in a bank's safe deposit box and keep photocopies at home.

 TIME-SAVING TIP   INFLUENCE   FOCUS

Travel

CAR

630. Airport servicing Some airports now have garages that will service your car while you are away on your trip. This spares you bringing the car to your garage and retrieving it, and also finding and paying for parking at the airport. Ask for directions at one of the airport filling stations.

631. Breakdowns Each time you have your car in for maintenance, have the pressure in your spare tire checked. If you need to change a tire, you will probably find that the jack and wrenches that came with your car are hard to use. Buy a pump jack and an X wrench. Also carry a can of sealant for flat tires. And get battery cables in case you need to jump start your car or someone else's.

632. Carpool When commuting, consider carpooling. Some cities have a special speed lane for cars with at least two or three passengers. City Hall will give you a number to call to inquire about carpools in your neighborhood, or watch for highway signs offering information. There may also be a service at your workplace.

633. Change Carry change in your car for meters and tolls. Buy rolls of coins on your annual trip to the bank; store them at home and supply the coin case in the car as necessary. Drop your spare change in receptacles when you hang up your clothes. Use those coins to supply the car as well. (See Travel-Car-Toll booths.)

634. Commuting If you are among those who stop at a gym on your way to work, consider joining a gym near your office, not near your home; in that way, you are likely to encounter less traffic during much of your commute.

635. Commuting We are told that Angelinos find that the freeway is where they spend the two calmest and most rewarding hours of their daily lives. We think there's got to be a better place for private time than behind the wheel of a car stuck in traffic. Our suggestion: Talk with your family about creating a private space at home that they will not intrude on during certain times, for example, in the hour after you return home. Then, see if you can shorten your commuting time by changing your mode of transportation, route to work, working hours, location of your work, or even the location of your home.

636. Commuting When choosing a home and when choosing an employer, analyze your commuting time (on foot, by car, train, bus, etc.) and give that its appropriate weight.

Heed E. B. White's warning to a commuter:

DO YOU WANT TO SPEND YOUR LIFE
RIDING TO AND FROM YOUR WIFE?

If you don't like to be kept waiting for ten minutes at work, will you really be happy waiting ten times as long (or more) every day in your car?

637. Deliveries Whether or not you have a car, consider getting a charge account with a taxi company (or a delivery service) that will fetch and deliver things for you (packages, laundry, etc.). A taxi can drop off and pick up your kids for appointments, too.

638. Doubling up

If you spend periods as long as a half hour in your car, consider buying audio tapes that put the time to good use. While you drive, you can study a foreign language, listen to poetry or music, hear an author reading from his or her work, or take audio book courses. Check out the collection at your bookstore or library.

You can also dictate correspondence or notes to yourself using a portable tape recorder (we like the Sony Pressman); review the day's events and plan those of the following day; place telephone calls with a car or cellular phone.

639. Driver No question, operating a car takes up a lot of
time: There's buying the car in the first place, then maintenance, fueling, repairs, taxes, licenses, inspections, parking, parking permits at home and work, parking tickets, traffic violations, insurance purchasing, insurance claims, selling or trading the car—and more.

Consider paying someone to do these things for you—a college student, a driver if you can afford one, or a housekeeper, assistant or cook if you have regular help. You may come out money ahead if you put the time saved to work, and certainly your nerves will be less frayed.

Do you really need a car? You may save time and money going without one. Perhaps you can carpool to work, use public transportation on occasion, walk or ride a bicycle more often, take taxis, and rent a car for weekend excursions.

640. Drive-through You can perform many errands
while in your car without getting out of it. Those include banking, getting fast food, a stop at the dry cleaners, beverage purchases and more. Consider making those stops while you are on another errand with your car. Using a drive-through service is faster than parking, entering the place of business and waiting in line.

641. Extra key You can buy a car key that is as flat as a credit card to keep in your wallet—in case you forget your keys or lock them in your car. Ask your car dealer or locksmith.

642. Filling up the tank Don't make a separate trip to put gas in your car. Seize the opportunity to fill up when you pass a gas station without a line. Stations that accept credit cards at the pump are time savers. Most gas stations have shorter lines in the evening, after the work day is over.

643. Insurance Accidents will happen. When they do, you can save time by using an accident reporting form that you carry in your glove compartment. You can get the forms from your insurance agent but some auto supply stores and car dealers provide them in the shape of an envelope to hold your important papers such as car registration. Keep a ball point pen in there, too.

644. Maintenance Although most garages stick a label somewhere in your car indicating when your next service is due, sometimes they forget or the label becomes illegible. Put reminders in your calendar for oil change and general mainte-nance. Consult your car manual to find the right intervals for servicing. Proving you respected those intervals can be important when trading or selling your car.

645. Maps Keep city maps and highway maps in your car. Few experiences are more terrifying for the city-dweller than try-ing to find an address in the helter-skelter streets of suburbia, so if you're a city-dweller get a suburban street guide as well. Be sure the indexes are readable using only available light in the car.

It's a good practice to have additional sets of maps at home and work, perhaps with an accent marker handy, so you can plan itiner-aries comfortably ahead of time. The last thing you want is to wan-der around looking for an open gas station to give you directions.

The American Automobile Association (AAA) provides mem-bers with maps and specialized map-booklets that chart the best

TIME-SAVING TIP

INFLUENCE

FOCUS

route to your destination, along with tour books and special deals on flights, cars, and hotels. (www.aaa.com)

646. Minimizing stops If you want to save time when traveling considerable distances by car, take along prepared meals, snacks, water, etc. That way, you will keep stops to a minimum—breaks for the bathroom, for stretching, and for staying alert.

647. Parked car location Attach a colorful piece of ribbon to your car antenna to spot the car more easily when retrieving it from a large parking lot or structure. Remote control door locks, a security feature, chirp when activated with a remote "beeper," making it easier to find the car. You can also try to remember a landmark or aisle number. If you have a dashboard pad, as we recommend, you can write the location on the parking ticket or on a slip of paper that you take with you when you leave the car.

648. Parking If you can afford a car, you can probably afford parking lots—they will be a small fraction of your annual car expense. If you value your time, why waste it driving in circles looking for a meter or free space, when there's a paying lot nearby? Pull in and save on stress and gasoline, too.

649. Parking If you park on streets that have weekly street cleaning or alternate-side parking for another reason, place a recurrent reminder in your calendar for the night before. A towed car is a terrible waste of time and money.

650. Parking lot You will save time parking by using valet parking and parking lots with attendants who park your car. Ask the valet or attendant not to garage the car or surround it in the back of the lot, but to keep it handy. Most will oblige when they can, particularly if tipped. When arriving at a parking lot, pull up to the attendant or booth and get out of the car at once,

BENEFITS   BURDENS   BALANCE

so you will not be asked to park your car. If the lot requires a deposit, take out your wallet promptly and say "the keys are in the car." If you are in a rush, act like it and say so.

 651. Parking plans Let the availability of parking influence your choice of where to shop and eat. When you plan ahead of time, favor places that have reserved or valet parking and tell them so. If you are in the car running errands, consider choosing a place to shop or eat for its convenience and the availability of parking at the site or nearby.

 652. Parking reserved If parking is not to steal a lot of your valuable time, you need a place of your own to park at home and one at work. If you live in a building that does not provide reserved parking, you will have to find a spot for rent; you may need to prepare a flyer to put on parked cars in your neighborhood, or you can place an ad in the neighborhood paper.

Some short-sighted employers provide their employees only with "hunting permits" that authorize them to hunt for a parking spot in the company's lot. Sometimes you can see employees idling and fuming just like their cars while they wait for a spot to open up. If you value your time, you'll investigate the possibility of renting a reserved space nearby. Also see our tip on carpooling.

 653. Parking structure Don't park in a parking structure: It's best to avoid parking structures entirely since they waste a lot of your time: First, you comb the structure looking for a space, park, and take the stairs or elevator down. Then, on your return, you take the stairs or elevator up, retrace your path in the car, and wait on line to pay.

- Take a cab.
- Take public transportation if it is frequent and fast.
- Walk if your destination is nearby.
- Use valet parking if available.
- Use a parking lot.
- Drive past your destination looking for parking spots close by.
- Have someone drop you off or pick you up or both.

TIME-SAVING TIP

INFLUENCE

FOCUS

654. Parking structure In parking structures, a sign
that says the level is FULL commonly means there is space available on that level, so you should enter and look for a space. That's because there is always some delay in resetting the signage, so some cars leave the level while cars entering the structure continue to pass that level up. Depending on the structure and time of day, there is some risk that the level really is full, but try our advice a few times and see how you do.

Similarly, parking structures that announce they are FULL at the entrance generally are not full and you should feel free to enter if you can and look for a space. If you must use a structure it's best to keep to the levels closest to the entrance, where all the steps involved are faster, and there are fewer cars that can line up ahead of you to pay when leaving.

It's foolhardy to use a parking structure when you know that everyone will be leaving at about the same time—for example, after a movie or show.

655. Parking, scouting If you know you will be driving to a nearby destination—for example, if you have an appointment—it may be worthwhile to drive past the site when on an errand to scout for the parking you will need. Confident that there's parking nearby, you can leave for the appointment much later, avoid anxious minutes searching, and arrive on time.

If you remember to ask about parking when making the appointment in the first place, you may not even have to reconnoiter.

656. Permits Put a recurring annual reminder in your calendar for each of the stickers that you must renew—registration, inspection, parking, and others. Set the date for a few weeks before the deadline, so you can schedule the chore conveniently.

657. Purchasing If you live or work in the city, you can save time (and money) by buying a smaller car rather than a larger one: You will find more parking spaces on the street.

You can reduce the time you spend on maintenance and repairs by choosing a car with low repair rates; consult Consumer

BENEFITS

BURDENS

BALANCE

Reports annual car buying issue. Favor car dealers who are closer to your home.

Avoid insurance hassles and worse by avoiding cars with high risk of theft. Your local police department, insurance agent, or state department of motor vehicles can give you a list of cars stolen most often in your area, and there's a national list in Consumer Reports. Be sure to purchase anti-theft devices to reduce your risk and save on insurance costs.

When purchasing a car, you will be told that you must make trips to your insurance agent, the registry of motor vehicles, the bank to get a certified check, the dealership to pay the balance, and finally the dealership again to get the car. All lies. The dealer has runners who will do all the errands (for a nominal charge) and your salesperson will be glad to deliver your car.

○ 658. Rental

- Some car rental companies will deliver a car to your door, and recover it there after your trip. Example: Enterprise (1-800-325-8007).
- Most car rental companies offer preferred services, either to frequent renters or for a fee. These often allow you to pick up your car without having to check in at a counter. For example: Hertz (1-800-654-3131).
- Many will have the rental contract complete before your arrival; you merely sign and go.
- Ask your travel agent to select a company that provides these services, but avoid one, if you can, that is a lengthy bus ride away from the airport. That not only wastes time, but you might miss your return flight while waiting at the drop-off point for the company's van to take you back to the airport.
- When possible, prefer rental companies at the airport that allow you to drop your car off at walking distance from the terminal.
- Many companies offer substantial discounts on weekends— except during periods of heavy demand such as holiday weekends.
- Some companies will rent you a car with a computerized display of your route and area roads and streets. This helpful device also provides information about traffic flow and alternate routes.

TIME-SAVING TIP

INFLUENCE

FOCUS

659. Speeding Respect the highway and city speed limits. ⏱
It's often safer to do so. Your time savings from speeding is likely
to be small, and if you are stopped by the police, you'll waste a lot
of time. Increasing your speed from 55 to 65 mph, for example,
will save you only nine minutes on an hour's drive. In town, traffic lights are often synchronized for the posted speed, so there is
no time to be gained by driving faster.

Nevertheless, some drivers exceed the speed limits, especially
on roads whose limits were reduced unrealistically in the era
when government was eager for fuel conservation. Radar detectors
are available to reduce your chances of being stopped for speeding
by the police. Before buying one, be sure it is legal in your state.
A popular model is the Escort passport (1-800-543-1608).

660. Toll booths The only thing to be said for toll booths ⏱
is that they provide politicians with paltry political patronage to
distribute. Those politicians are finally realizing, however, that
their constituents would like to strangle them as they sit in needlessly backed up traffic. In some cities toll booths are coming
down, while in others they are being converted to non-stop
booths that use bar code scanners to bill drivers.

E-ZPass customers carry a chip in their cars that transmits information about their vehicle to a computer in the lane they pass
through; the toll is then deducted from a prepaid account. For a
list of E-ZPass sites, consult www.EZPass.com. Some drivers
caught in needless toll booth bottlenecks save time by driving in
the "breakdown" or service lane. Don't do it. The lane may end
abruptly, police may issue a ticket, or an emergency vehicle may
need to get through while other drivers block your cutting in.

If someone coming out of the breakdown lane is trying to pull
in ahead of you, why not be courteous—it will only lengthen
your wait by a few seconds—the time it would have taken them
to pay the toll.

661. Traffic Check on traffic conditions before getting in ⏱
the car as well as on the road. You may decide beforehand to
choose an alternate form of transportation or an alternate route.
Some radio stations provide frequent travel advisories. In many
cities you can call for that information as well; check with the

BENEFITS

BURDENS

BALANCE

traffic department or local police. If you have a cellular phone, ask your service provider what number to call for traffic advisories. You may also find one for your area on the Web. Check out www.smarttraveler.com.

 662. Traffic lights Impatient at slow traffic lights? Jot some notes on your dashboard pad. Place a call with your car phone. Review the rest of your itinerary. Think about what will happen at your destination. Listen to an audio book. Consider: Would a different route have avoided this light? Should I be using another means of transportation? Is the trip necessary?

 663. Traffic lights Unless a traffic sign prohibits it, you are free to turn right on red after stopping in most states (the Environmental Protection Agency made that rule years ago). Many drivers do not know that it is also legal in most states to turn left on red from a one-way street into a one-way street.

In some cities, "no right on red" signs have been posted excessively or are relics of an earlier time, and many drivers proceed after stopping when neither pedestrians nor police nor other cars are in sight. However, we do not advocate breaking the law.

 664. What to have in your car Many of these items are available from your local automotive supply store, or from Sporty's automotive supply catalogue (1-800-543-8633).

GLOVE COMPARTMENT
Car manual
De-icer
Dust cloth
Eyeglasses (spare)
First-aid kit
Flashlight
Insurance card
Maps
Nail file
Portable electric razor
Pressure gauge

 TIME-SAVING TIP   INFLUENCE   FOCUS

Registration
Service booklet
Sunglasses
Towing club membership

TRUNK
Blanket
Chains
Emergency flag
Flares
Gas can
Ice scraper-brush
Jack
Jumper cables
Kitty litter (for traction)
Oil
Rags
Reflectors
Shovel
Spare tire
Tire inflation aerosol
Window cleaner & paper towels
Wrench

INTERIOR
Change for tolls
Dashboard pad
Trash bag
Tissues
Telescoping umbrella

PACKING

665. Customs Take documents on your trip showing which equipment in your possession (computer, camera, expensive watch, etc.) was purchased before leaving the U.S. If you have time to stop at customs with your bags, they will give you a

BENEFITS

BURDENS

BALANCE

document verifying that you had those items before departure. If you are stopped by customs on return and cannot prove that you purchased those things in the U.S., you may lose some time and money paying an import tax on items whose country of origin you cannot prove.

666. Digital watch When traveling across time zones, it is convenient to wear a watch and pack an alarm clock that can readily be reset to the new time. Digital alarms have the further advantage that they can be set for the exact amount of time available for an activity or catnap.

667. Documents Make photocopies of your important documents (passport, driver's license, credit cards) and take them along. If the original is stolen or lost, the photocopy will greatly speed reporting the lost document and getting a new one.

668. Doubling up When taking public transportation, always carry a book, periodical, or other material to read, as well as a pocket size jotter (pad & pencil) to make notes and lists, record ideas.

669. Emergency For many businesspeople and others it is prudent to have an emergency carry-on suitcase ready for hasty departures. It should include toiletries and medications and clothing for a day or two. A friend, relative or employee can bring or send the already packed suitcase to the office or airport.

670. Ironing Hotels charge shocking sums to press clothing, and they may leave you in your underwear waiting for hours for your suit or dress to return. Hang your wrinkled clothes in the bathroom; turn on the shower with hot water, and steam iron your clothes (close the door). There are also lightweight suit and dress steamers sold in travel shops and advertised in airplane magazines. Choose one that works on 220 volts as well as 110 volts, if you travel abroad.

TIME-SAVING TIP

INFLUENCE

FOCUS

Your clothes will come out of the suitcase less wrinkled in the first place if you pack them between layers of material. For this purpose, save the plastic bags that your dry cleaning is returned in—they make an excellent wrinkle guard.

671. Laptop computer
If you are taking along your laptop computer, review the following list of must-haves when packing:

- Fully charged batteries
- Power supply cord
- Extension cord
- Adapter plugs
- Telephone cable for modem
- Adapter plugs for phone jack

Some airlines now provide power for laptops in business and first class.

672. Luggage
Of course you will usually want to carry on your luggage when possible. The airlines provide large incentives to do so when they under-staff their ticket counters and require travelers who need to check baggage to wait in line at the counter. They provide further incentives to take carry-on when they lose checked bags or fail to put them on a connecting flight, and when they take a long time to get the bags off the plane and into your hands.

Instead of remedying the problems that have led a great many travelers to take carry-on, a few airlines have recently chosen to place further restrictions on carry-on. When booking your flights, ask your travel agent to tell you the carry-on restrictions. If you can avoid those airlines, so much the better.

With carry-on you can change your routing at the last minute, take advantage of cash awards for overbooking, and also have your things available to you en route.

You may have difficulty finding space for your carry-on in the plane, but if it is within the legal dimensions, the flight attendant will find a place for it. If your carry-on doesn't have wheels, you will have to lug it between the terminal and the gate.

BENEFITS   BURDENS   BALANCE

673. Luggage We like the TravelPro Rollaboard line (1-305-426-5996) of carry-on luggage, which has a retractable handle and wheels, and good stability. A wide selection of carry-on luggage is available at www.ebags.com. To go under the seat, your luggage cannot exceed 9 x 14 x 22 inches. To go into the overhead bin, it cannot exceed 10 x 14 x 36 inches. Airline restrictions may vary, however; ask your travel agent.

674. Packing List You don't want to forget to pack anything you will need at your destination, for it will cost you time to obtain it. Here is a comprehensive list of packing reminders. Adapt it to your needs. (Starred items are essential to pack for most trips, even short ones.)

CLOTHES
- Bathing cap
- Bathrobe
- Belt
- Blouse
- Boots
- Cap
- Coat
- Collar stays
- Cufflinks
- Dress
- Gloves
- Handbag
- Handkerchiefs
- Hat
- Jacket, outer
- Jacket, sport
- Jeans
- Jewelry
- Nightgown
- Pajamas
- Pants
- Pants, casual
- Pocketbook
- Raincoat
- Robe
- Sandals
- Scarf
- Shirts, dress
- Shirts, sport
- Shoes
- Shorts
- Skirt
- Sleep mask*
- Slippers
- Sneakers
- Socks, hose
- Suit
- Sunglasses*
- Sweater
- Sweater vest
- Sweatpants
- Sweatshirt
- Swim suit
- Tie
- Towel
- Umbrella
- Underwear
- Wallet
- Watch

FOR THE BEACH
- Beach bag
- Beach towel

TIME-SAVING TIP

INFLUENCE

FOCUS

Book
Bottle opener
Cap
Cards
Chair, folding
Eyeglasses (spare)
Fish bait
Flip-flops
Food
Matches
Money
Pencil/paper
Snorkel
Sunglasses
Sunglasses, Rx
Suntan oil
Swim suit
Talcum powder
Towel
Water

Hydrocortisone cream
Insect repellent
Laundry bag
Lipstick*
Makeup
Mirror
Moisturizer
Mouthwash
Nailboards*
Nail clippers
Nail polish*
Nick stick
Perfume, cologne
Plastic bags
Pre-electric shave
Prescriptions
Razor*
Sanitary pads or tampons
Shampoo
Shaving cream*
Soap
Spot removal pads
Sunburn ointment
Suntan oil
Suntan lotion
Swabs
Toothbrush*
Toothpaste*
Toothpicks
Towelettes
Woolite packets

TOILETRIES & OTHER NECESSITIES
After shave
Alcohol pads
Antacid*
Aspirin
Band-Aids
Batteries AA & AAA
Chapstick*
Comb/Brush*
Contraceptives
Cosmetics
Cuticle clippers
Cuticle scissors
Deodorant
Dental Floss
Diarrhea medication
Earplugs*
Hair Conditioner
Hairdryer*
Hairspray*
Hand cream

ACCESSORIES
Adapter plugs
Address book
Auto rental card
Boarding passes*
Briefcase
Business cards*
Business papers
Calculator
Calendar

BENEFITS

BURDENS

BALANCE

Camera
Camera batteries
Camera film
Camera lenses
Carryall bag
Cash*
Cash foreign
Cash machine codes
Cellular phone
Checkbook
Coin purse
Computer
Correspondence
Credit cards
Dictionaries / phrase books
"Do not disturb" sign
Electricity Converter
Expense booklets
Eyeglasses*
Frequent flyer numbers
Gifts
Hangers
House key
Itinerary
Keys
Maps

Passport & photocopy
Pencils
Pen
Pen refills
Phone calling codes
Plane tickets*
Pocket pad
Radar detector
Reading matter
Restaurant guide
Resume
Sewing kit
Shoe polish
Stamps
Tape recorder
Telephone list—Foreign
Telephone list—US *
Travel alarm
Travel guides
Travel iron
Traveler's checks
Vaccination cards
Visas
Walkman
Writing paper

And before you leave your home or office, call to suspend newspaper delivery and change your phone message if you need to.

⏱ **675. Toiletries** Lightweight see-through bags for carrying toiletries—and many more practical travel items—are available from Magellan's (1-800-962-4943) and Travel Smith (1-800-950-1600). If you carry more toiletries than one bag will hold, use two but distribute items according to some principle, for example, all "wet" items in one bag, dry in the other. If you restock these bags after each trip, they will always be ready to go, and your packing time will be much reduced.

TIME-SAVING TIP

INFLUENCE

FOCUS

676. Travel light We asked our travel agent for the single most important tip to give travelers and she responded, "Pack light." Experienced travelers generally travel light, especially as carry-on luggage will not hold a great deal. Consider wearing the dressier outfit for your trip, including comfortable dress shoes. Pack toiletries, informal clothes, papers, underwear and such. Take only clothes that can be matched to each other: a solid light blue shirt rather than a striped red one. Take drip-dry clothing when possible. Only take clothing you will need, rather than clothing you might need. Lightweight wools and knits pack well. Never pack important papers or your sole supply of medicines for the trip.

PLANE

677. Airport transfers

- If you have a choice of airports for departures and arrivals, be sure to ask your travel agent which has the shortest travel time to and from the airport.
- Also ask about the best mode of transportation; in some cities there's a train to and from the airport that is faster than a taxi, especially during rush hour.
- "Gypsy" drivers may approach you as you leave the arrivals terminal in some airports, such as New York's JFK. You may want to take them up on their offer of limousine service to the city, especially if there is a queue for taxicabs, but be sure to agree on the cost beforehand and ask where their car is parked; if it is in a structure, you will have to wait.
- When practical, avoid flight schedules that require you to go to and from the airport during a rush hour in which traffic is flowing in the same direction that you are. For example, when traveling between two city centers, you want to avoid late afternoon departures and early morning arrivals. Estimated driving times between the airport and downtown (Caution: these vary depending on time of day):

BENEFITS

BURDENS

BALANCE

AIRPORT	MINUTES DRIVING TIME
Atlanta	30
Chicago O'Hare	45
Dallas	25
Denver	35
Los Angeles	30
Miami	30
New York JFK	40
San Francisco	25
London Gatwick	60
London Heathrow	45
Paris De Gaulle	45
Paris Orly	30
Tokyo Haneda	60

⏱ 678. Airports

- Before leaving on a plane trip, it is prudent to call the airport or airline to make sure your flight is leaving as scheduled.

- Arriving at airports unnecessarily early is an irritating waste of time, though the airlines, who could not care less about your time, would like you to arrive hours in advance. The time-conscious person arrives at the airport with enough time to accomplish all necessary tasks—but not more time than that.

- Subtract from your departure time an estimate of the time to the airport (consult the table above or ask your travel agent). Subtract ten minutes for understaffed baggage screening and long corridors to the gate. Subtract another ten minutes so that the airline does not give away your seat. And there you have the time you should leave for the airport.

- The airlines hate it, but some travelers book on two consecutive flights, as a precaution. You probably would have to purchase two tickets and hope you could refund the one you don't use.

- If you must clear U.S. customs and immigration, add 5 minutes outbound and 30 minutes inbound.

- Whenever possible arrive at the airport with boarding passes, carry-on luggage, and work to do or something to read during the delays.

TIME-SAVING TIP

INFLUENCE

FOCUS

👍 Working at home or at the office until close to flight time is often better than trying to do something useful in an airport waiting area.

👎 If you cut it close and there are unexpected delays en route, you may miss your flight.

679. Baggage 🕐

- Place an identification tag on your baggage. Choose a large, distinctive outside tag, as many pieces of luggage look alike. A colored piece of yarn on the handle will also help to mark your bag as your own.
- Also put a tag on the inside of the bag, with your home and destination addresses.
- This is wise advice even if you are using carry-on luggage, for a fellow traveler may take yours from the overhead bin if it is not distinctive. Similarly, your bag may be confused with others when checking into or out of a hotel. ·
- If you must check baggage, verify that the agent has attached a tag with the correct destination.

680. Baggage claim If you have checked luggage and 🕐 have reserved a rental car, on arrival go first to the car rental desk in the baggage claim area (if there is one) and take care of the paperwork. If you pass a security officer, tell them you will be coming back for your bags. By the time you do, your luggage should have arrived but be sure that its appearance is distinctive, so no one takes your bags before you do.

681. Boarding Don't rush to the boarding gate like every- 🕐 one else when boarding begins. After all, you don't want to stand in line. Continue what you're doing while passengers board; you have a reserved seat.

If you will need to put your carry-on luggage in the overhead compartment, however, then it's prudent not to be among the last to board for you may find the compartments near your seat are full.

First-class passengers and those with enough frequent flyer miles to qualify for special treatment are invited to board at their convenience. If you are among them, you may board at first call,

BENEFITS

BURDENS

BALANCE

get settled in your seat without waiting for others to clear the aisle, and resume what you were doing.

 682. Boarding passes Get a seat assignment and boarding pass when you buy your ticket. If it's too far in advance, at least get the return assignment and pass when you check in outbound. This provides you with more choice of seating and, in airports that do not require you to present photo ID, you can skip the check-in lines entirely both at the ticket counter and at the gate.

 683. Booking You should have your travel agent do any telephoning to airlines that is necessary. If for some reason you must call an airline and they put you on hold, as they often do nowadays, the civic-minded thing to do is hang up and, when possible, avoid booking with that airline. If enough of us hang up, they may hire more agents.

If you really need to talk to that airline right now, call information and get their number in another city where access may actually be easier than the city you are calling from.

 684. Cancellation If your plane flight is seriously delayed or canceled at the last minute, chances are that many passengers like you will rush to the airline ticket counter and stand in line for new reservations.

Since you never wait in line, call your travel agent or the airline's reservation number on your cell phone or from the nearest payphone, so you can continue to hear announcements at the gate. You will have a better chance of securing a seat on the next flight.

Ask your travel agent for airline phone numbers that will connect you directly with a live person and not a recording.

 685. Choice of seat If you're traveling in economy class, pick an aisle seat with your writing arm on the aisle side. Of course, you may have to get up to let another passenger out but you will be more comfortable writing or typing and you won't have to ask to be excused if you want to leave your seat.

If you select a seat forward in the plane, you will get to it sooner and disembark sooner.

TIME-SAVING TIP

INFLUENCE

FOCUS

686. Connections Fly nonstop whenever possible—or at least direct; that is, without changing planes. If you must change planes, prefer airports that

- are less crowded
- have shorter distances between gates
- offer more connecting service to your destination (in case you miss your connection).

Avoid when possible these eight busiest U.S. airports:

- Chicago O'Hare
- Atlanta
- Dallas/Ft. Worth
- Los Angeles International
- San Francisco
- Miami
- Denver
- New York JFK

And these international airports:

- London Heathrow
- Tokyo Haneda
- Paris Charles De Gaulle Terminal 1

For London, try Gatwick airport instead (there's direct train service to the city).

For Paris, try Orly airport (it's also closer to the city than Charles de Gaulle airport). Look for these red flags and request a different routing when they appear (ask your travel agent):

- The official connection time is too short (or too long).
- Your first flight often arrives late at the connecting airport (according to the on-time record for that flight posted on your travel agent's computer screen).
- Your first flight does not originate where you board.
- If you miss your connection, there's a long wait for the next flight.

Flying nonstop or direct, you have half the chance of a canceled or delayed flight; travel time is shorter; you and your baggage are more likely to arrive on time. If you use less crowded airports, you are more likely to reach your destination on time.

BENEFITS

BURDENS

BALANCE

It takes longer to book your flight when you dispute the computer routing. Using alternative airports may prolong your flight time.

687. Flight checklist

Plane transportation checklist:

- Are the date & time correct on tickets?
- Do I have boarding passes with seats specified?
- Are the seats non-smoking?
- Do I have a seat that reclines?
- Am I seated in an emergency exit row?
- Are my traveling companions adjacent?
- Did I enter departure and arrival times in my calendar?
- Did I enter flights in frequent flyer log?
- Did I request special meals?
- Is frequent flyer number entered on boarding pass?
- Are return date & time correct?
- Is there enough time to make connecting flights? Is this an international connection?
- Am I eligible for upgrade or do I want to purchase one?
- Is ground transportation reserved as necessary?
- Check flight durations: am I routed the shortest way? Did I pack enough leisure reading or work to do?
- Do I have local currency?
- If renting a car, does agency have my frequent flyer number?
- Do I have car rental reservation, desk location, and necessary maps?
- If the city has more than one airport, is it clear which are the airports of arrival and departure?
- Do I have my passport, visa and immunization card if necessary?
- Am I avoiding the peak hours for traffic to and from the airport?
- Have flight times changed since I last informed my host?

688. Flight information Unless your mother is coming for a visit, think twice before offering to pick someone up at the airport.

- It may take you a long time to get there, especially if it is rush hour, and you may even keep your guests waiting.

TIME-SAVING TIP

INFLUENCE

FOCUS

- Increasingly, airports do not let you wait in your car near the terminal, so you must park at a distance and walk. You may have to help lug your guests' baggage back to your car.
- It is easy to miss your guest at the airport, especially as security now prevents you from going to the gate, and monitors do not give up-to-the-minute flight arrival information.
- If you must meet someone at the airport, it may be easier to meet them curbside at the Departures level, which is often less crowded than Arrivals.
- If you leave for the airport without checking on the time of arrival of the flight you are meeting, you may cool your heels there for hours. But if you call to find out that time, you'll probably be put on hold. Some airlines, however, do provide automated flight information by telephone or on the Internet.
- Why not order a "town car" from a limousine service to pick up your guests? They will almost surely arrive sooner than if you fetch them yourself and the cost is little more than a taxi. (Look in the Yellow Pages under "limousines.")
- Many cities now have door-to-door van services that are less expensive than a reserved town car but usually take somewhat longer. Call in advance to determine whether they limit the number of passengers per van and how large a geographic area a single van covers, as it's possible to spend several hours driving around your destination city while other passengers get dropped off first.

689. Foreign travel Consular information sheets are available for all countries, which provide currency regulations, health conditions, areas of political instability and of crime, and the addresses of U.S. embassies and consulates. Call the State Department at (202) 647-5225 or on the Internet: http://travel.state.gov. Health information in more detail, including recommended inoculations, can be had from the Centers for Disease Control: (404) 332-4559.

690. Frequent flyers As airlines sometimes fail to credit frequent flyer accounts, especially when travel is overseas on a partner airline, it is good practice to save your boarding passes and ticket stub and to check your frequent flyer statement when it arrives.

BENEFITS   BURDENS   BALANCE

691. Jet lag

- If you detest jet lag, you might take a tip from the birds and, when you have a choice, migrate within the same time zone.
- Body rhythms are less disrupted by extending your waking hours (traveling westbound) than by starting a new day several hours too early (traveling eastbound). When possible, choose a flight that arrives at a time close to your bedtime.
- Expect that it will take you one day to adjust to the time change for each two hours of time difference. Relax on your arrival and ease into the new schedule.
- See our tips below on getting sleep during the flight.

692. Lounges

- If your airline ticket qualifies you for the first class or business class lounge, you may find the facilities there adequate for what you want to do (phone calls, faxes, reading and typing) and thus you can arrive at the airport earlier with less loss of productive time.
- The lounge is also a welcome haven when there are unexpected delays. Check out the cost of annual lounge membership if you travel on a particular airline repeatedly.

693. Meals

Not only are most meals on airplanes appalling and getting worse, they are a waste of time, for they take up the space in front of you, preventing you from working and even reading comfortably. Order a special meal when you make your reservation and you are likely to be served first. When you are done eating, ask the flight attendant to remove your tray, or place it on the floor in front of your seat.

Or pack a snack and bring it on board with you. It will probably be better food and you can put the remains of your meal back in the bag and continue your work while those around you wait to have their trays removed.

If you are traveling overnight, you'd be wise to eat before going to the airport, and inform the flight attendant as you take your seat that you want to skip the drinks and meal in order to sleep. In first and business class, you can ask to be served your entire meal at once, as soon as the flight climbs to cruising altitude. This request is routine and will allow you to get to sleep or work sooner.

TIME-SAVING TIP

INFLUENCE   FOCUS

694. Meetings If you fly to see a partner or client for just a day, consider meeting him or her at their airport, where there are often lounges set aside for the purpose, or in an airport hotel. You will gain productive time by not traveling into the city and back to the airport.

695. Office in the air

- For people who want to get serious work done en route and at their destination, there's no substitute for a laptop computer. You can use it to consult your calendar, your contacts list, and any files you may need. You can also take notes, prepare correspondence, send and receive faxes, and check your email.
- Avoid the bulky and heavy laptops; get a light sub-notebook; for example, the IBM ThinkPad 560 (1-800-426-2968).
- You may be satisfied to take pen or pencil and paper if the flight is short, but it's a waste of time to write extensively by hand and then later enter it on a computer.
- Do not travel with fountain pens. They often leak once you are airborne and can seriously stain your clothes.

696. Sleep
You will sleep better on the plane if you

- Inform the flight attendant of your plan.
- Wear a sleep mask. You can purchase them from Flents (1-203-866-2581).
- Wear ear plugs. The most effective are EAR brand available from many pharmacies and from Sporty's shops (1-800-543-8633).
- Take a relaxant or sleeping pill. (Ask your pharmacist or doctor.)
- Keep your buckled seat belt visible to the flight attendants, so they will not need to wake you to see if it is fastened.
- Fly business or first class when possible. Fully reclining seats wide enough for an adult, footrests, and fewer noisy children than in coach all contribute to better conditions for sleep.
- Seize an empty row in coach after the doors close and spread out to defend your territory. Place extra blankets and pillows on adjacent seats. When the seat belt sign is turned off, raise the seat dividers, press all but one of the belts into

BENEFITS BURDENS BALANCE

the slots between the seats, make a bed, fasten a seatbelt around you so the buckle is visible, and sleep tight.

697. Space With all the various ways airlines are using the Internet, the number of unsold seats is down and full flights are becoming nearly standard. Nevertheless, if you have a choice of the day or time when you travel, ask your travel agent which flights are less crowded. You might be able to spread out a little and do some work or sleep on a less crowded flight.

698. Upgrading Consider traveling business or first class. You will find that you can get much more accomplished in a seat that is wider than you are and with your knees lower than your chin. You can also board and leave the plane sooner and you will arrive less fatigued. Upgrading often costs less than you might think, especially if you must otherwise pay the full coach fare. Upgrading can cost you nothing if you join the airline's frequent flyer club.

PLANNING

699. Business trip checklist Use this checklist to be sure you have all the information you need when planning a business trip. Leave a copy with your family, another in the office, and take one with you. If you need a phone number or address at the last minute, it will be handy.

Host person or organization:
Street address, city, state zip code:
Departure city and date:
Return city and date:
Nature of the event:
Duration of the event:
Contact name:
Contact title:
Contact address:
Work Phone: (   ) Fax: (   )

TIME-SAVING TIP

INFLUENCE

FOCUS

Home Phone: (　　　　　) Fax: (　　　　　)
email address:
Location of event:
Address and telephone:
Time of event:
Suggested airport for arrival:
Estimated time from airport to site:
On arrival at the airport, go to:
Preferred day and time of arrival at destination:
Preferred mode of transportation from airport to location:
Preferred day and time of departure from destination:
Expected size of audience or group:
Makeup of audience or group:
Name, address and telephone number of hotel or other
　　accommodation:
Telephone contact for day of travel in case of emergency:
Person to whom documents should be sent in advance:
Name:
Address:
Work Phone: (　　　　　) Fax: (　　　　　)

700. Choices—long haul

Think twice before you choose your mode of transportation for long trips. If you time it door to door, the train may be faster than the plane. Going by car allows you to leave and return at will, and it provides one mode of transportation for the entire trip. And you can transport a lot of clothing or other items. But you get much less work done driving or riding in a car than sitting in a train or plane.

701. Choices—short haul

Here are some alternatives to driving short distances that may save you time depending on the situation.

- Walking. No traffic slowdown, no hassle parking, no theft, it's healthy, too. But you can transport only light objects and it takes more time.
- Bicycling. Not much affected by traffic, little hassle parking, much faster than walking, also healthy. Can transport moderate weight materials. Can be dangerous navigating through traffic.

BENEFITS

BURDENS

BALANCE

- In-line roller blades. Unaffected by traffic, no need for parking, very fast, but somewhat dangerous. Not appropriate for formal occasions.
- Scooter. A favored form of personal transport in many European cities. Moves through traffic faster than a car but more dangerous in the city. Easier to park.
- Public transport. No parking problem and you can read while you travel. But service may be infrequent and stops far from your destination. Can be dangerous in some cities.

702. Expense reports Take along a pre-printed form to record expenses or record them on your laptop. You are less likely to overlook expenses if you record them frequently and keep receipts together in an envelope.

703. Fare—have it ready Stock up on tokens or tickets in advance, so you will not be caught without them nor have to wait on line to purchase them.

704. Foreign currency Don't want to wait in line to change currency at your foreign destination? Order the currency you will need at a bank or a currency office in your own country before you travel. If you have an American Express card, you can obtain foreign currency by mail (1-800-414-6914). Most major domestic airports have ATM machines that disburse foreign currency. It is more economical to use a debit card than a credit card for that transaction. Large amounts of foreign currency, however, usually cost less at the foreign destination. That's because the cost of money generally follows the law of supply and demand, and the supply of foreign currency is greater in the foreign country.

705. Hotel booking When booking your hotel room, ask for a room on the lower floors. You will spend less time waiting for, and riding in, elevators. You might even decide to take the stairs, to get a little exercise.

TIME-SAVING TIP   INFLUENCE   FOCUS

706. Hotel checklist You can save considerable time if you do not overlook anything when booking your hotel. Here is a list of reminders of topics to mention:

- Arrival date and time.
- Departure date and time.
- Early arrival, book prior night?
- Number of nights.
- Single or double.
- Type of bed.
- Private bath and shower.
- View desired.
- High or low floor desired.
- Quiet preferred.
- Air conditioning.
- Construction in progress?
- Health facilities; is pool open?
- Nonsmoking if desired.
- Discount packages.
- Breakfast included?
- Provision for late departures?
- Deposit required?
- Prices, tax, service charges.
- Provide credit card number.
- Confirmation number.
- Frequent flyer mileage credit.
- Give your fax & phone number.
- Ask their fax & phone number.

707. Hotel check-out time Most hotels require you to check out by noon. If you think you may need more time, ask for an extension of an hour or two when booking the room or when checking in; it will usually be granted without charge. This will also help you avoid lines when checking out if, for some reason, you do not use express check-out.

708. Meals Meetings in restaurants take longer than neces- sary and, because of distractions, are often less productive. To maximize your working time on a business trip, order breakfast or a snack served in your room.

BENEFITS   BURDENS   BALANCE

If your purpose, however, is to socialize, then dining out (especially on an expense account) is a nice way to do it.

○ **709. Off peak** When planning a holiday, ask yourself if it is absolutely necessary that you travel when everyone else does. The waits are longer; transportation and hotel costs are higher. If you travel regularly to a destination, familiarize yourself with the peak travel times and try to arrange your schedule to travel at off hours.

⊛ **710. Remain motionless** It is amazing how much needless running around you can avoid by simply declining to budge. A business contact asks you fly to Chicago to solve a problem. Think telephone, teleconferencing, and tell-a-subordinate. Likewise, one gathering of the clan can spare you several trips to see clan members. The same principle applies locally. Your bank tells you to stop in to get your traveler's checks. Refuse. The city parking office tells you to come in to get your permit. Refuse. Your appliance store tells you to come by and pick up your purchase. Refuse. After all, you don't want to wait on line, do you? Not to mention the time lost in travel and parking. Refuse politely. Explain that you are not able to stop in (leaving the vague implication that you are too ill or too busy or too old). Ask if there isn't some way that this can be done by fax, mail or a delivery service. There is. If the person you're talking to doesn't think so, ask for his or her supervisor.

○ **711. Reserved car** No one wants to wait in line for a taxi after returning from a trip. Especially if you plan to return during peak hours or expect bad weather, consider reserving a taxi or a "town car" from a limousine service. The cost is often less than you'd expect; for example, the ride from Boston's Logan airport to center city is about $26, including tip, as compared to $17 for a cab.

Be sure to give the service your flight information, so they will know if your flight is delayed; and take their phone number with you—just in case you don't see their car when you arrive.

 TIME-SAVING TIP   INFLUENCE   FOCUS

712. Travel agent It must be obvious by now that a good travel agent is a precious resource for time-conscious people who travel — so precious that it is worth investing some of your time in building a personal relationship with one. Once he or she knows your preferences and is committed to serving you well, you can be sure that a host of details will be taken care of — from entering your frequent flyer number to obtaining the shortest travel time and lowest fares. Incredibly, the service is free or at small cost to you. Select an agent by name that comes highly recommended by colleagues, friends or family. Our recommendation: Vicki Gelfund at Palm Travel (1-800-749-1900). Don't feel that you must choose an agent in your own community; tickets can be delivered by express mail or courier and enterprise calls (800 calls) cost you nothing.

A good travel agent will set up a personal profile for you, including your credit card and frequent flyer numbers, and your preferences for airlines, seating, meals, car rentals, etc.

713. Travel dates Tell a white lie about the day you are returning from a trip and make your actual return a day earlier. That will give you an appointment-free day to catch up on work, mail, and out-of-office calls that accumulated in your absence, to recover from the jet lag if any, and to re-acclimatize.

- Never lie to your secretary.
- Nor your spouse.

Response Form

If you have tips you'd like to share with us, please return this response form to: Marlowe & Company, 841 Broadway, 4th floor, New York, NY 10003 or fax: (212)614-7887. Of course, we'll acknowledge the tips we use. Time-wise citizens working togther could make life in our society a lot more pleasant and productive.

_____

_____

_____

_____

_____

_____

_____

_____

_____

_____

_____

_____

_____

Acknowledgments

We would like to thank the following people for all of their wonderful encouragement and assistance: Jean-Pierre Coffe, Janis Donnaud, Jason Freitas, Matthew Lore, Kelly Milligan, Franklin Phillip, and Adam Trotter.

About the Authors

A specialist in the psychology of language with a focal interest in Deaf people, Harlan Lane received bachelor's and master's degrees from Columbia University in 1958, a doctoral degree in psychology from Harvard University two years later, and a state doctorate in linguistics from the Sorbonne in 1973. For several years he was professor of psychology at the University of Michigan, where he founded and directed the Center for Research on Language and Language Behavior. He was a visiting professor of linguistics at the Sorbonne and then at the University of California San Diego. In 1974, he went to Northeastern University as Professor and Chairman of the Department of Psychology and soon thereafter founded the university's program of instruction in American Sign Language (ASL) and his own continuing program of sponsored research on ASL and Deaf culture. Dr. Lane is the author of numerous articles in professional journals concerning speech, hearing, and deafness, and of several books, among them, The Wild Boy of Aveyron: Foundations of Special Education, When the Mind Hears: A History of the Deaf, The Mask of Benevolence: Disabling the Deaf Community; and, with R. Hoffmeister and B. Bahan, A Journey into the Deaf-World. His honorary awards include the International Social Merit Award of the World Federation of the Deaf; the John D. and Catherine T. MacArthur Foundation Fellowship, the Distinguished Service and Literary Achievement Awards of the National Association of the Deaf, and the Order of Academic Palms from the French government. He is currently Distinguished University Professor at Northeastern University and Research Associate at the Massachusetts Institute of Technology.

Christian Wayser is a parliamentary attaché at the European Parliament. He has been a French antiques expert and collaborator with France's preeminent TV personality and guru of fine eating and living. He commutes between Paris, Brussels and Strasbourg.

Index

Page numbers in *italics* indicate recipes.

bedtime, 38
beeper, 59
behavior, 22, 30, 42, 178–9
belts, 173
Benson, Herbert, 163
Better Business Bureau, 46
beverages, 150, 151, 217
bicycling, 17, 49, 160, 161, 166,
        217, 241
bills, paying, 18, 68, 199, 210
binders, loose-leaf, 13, 69, 141, 191
birthdays, 50, 58, 147, 148, 182
blame, 24
Blazing Burritos, *118*
blinds, 169
board, erasable, 60, 134, 178
boarding, 233–4, 236
boards
    corporate, 8
    medical, 143
bonds, 104–5, 202
bookmarks, 152
books, 152–4
    at appointments, 38
    audio, 217, 224
    for beach, 229
    to borrow or buy, 31
    as gifts, 148
    organizing, 63, 153, 193
    for project, 42
    sexually explicit, 156
    for spare moments, 19, 50, 226
    supplies for, 208
    unused, 153, 170, 183
    websites, 96–7
bosses, 32, 35, 56, 65
bow tie, 172
brainstorming, 24, 28, 52
brands, 3, 12–13
Braun, 143
breakdowns, 215
breakfast, 53, 180, 182, 243

breaks, 16, 20, 36–7, 66, 166, 219
breathing, 163, 164
brevity, 72, 80
briefcase, 32, 59–60, 62, 200, 229
Brisk Beef Stir-fry, *118*
Broiled Chicken à la Diable, *130*
Brother, 75
Browne, Thomas, 170
Bruno, Giordano, 18
bulbs, light, 194
bulletin board, 60, 178, 208
Bullet Train Chicken, *118*
business, 52–69
    cards, 68, 200, 208, 229
    cooperative, 99
    literature, 50
    loyalty toward, 27
    retail, 80
    unfinished, 35
Business Book, 67, 200, 207
bus station, 48
Butter Sole, *130*

cable TV, 98, 145, 198
Caere Corporation, 91
caffeine, 158
calculator, 59, 68, 206, 208, 229
calendar, 37–8, 53–4, 60–1, 68,
        147, 208
    addresses and phone numbers
        in, 58
    alternate-side parking noted in,
        219
    carrying, 17, 28, 229
    checking air conditioners in, 195
    computerized, 31, 38, 42, 54, 58,
        60, 89, 92, 239
    deadlines, appointments and
        reminders in, 17, 36
    directions in, 148
    expected reply dates in, 210

of flight information, 236
software, 71, 90, 106
*see also specific kinds of
communication*
community activities and service,
140, 157
commuting, 11, 17, 38, 40, 41, 215,
216
see also telecommuting
complaints, 6–7, 9, 10, 45–6
CompUSA, 91
computer, 68, 89–112
addresses in, 58
backup, 5, 91, 92, 94, 106, 107,
111, 201, 207
configurations, 8
digital camera for, 176
environment for, 8
extra, 5
file folders list on, 203
fuse box and, 195
installation, 206
insurance for, 201
letters on, 18, 40
loans in, 31
pagers and, 85
phone numbers in, 85
postage from, 76
Post-it notes on, 67
of service providers, 9
speed, 93
standards for, 8
storage lists in, 186
tech support for, 13, 84, 97,
110–11, 153
of telecommuters, 65
time for, 111
To-Do lists on, 17, 30
username and password for, 6
user's manual for, 13
websites, 97–8
see also hardware; laptop; palm-

tops; software
concessions, 8
conciseness, *see* brevity
concurrency, 45, 50
condoms, 142, 156
conference calls, 52, 57, 81
confidence levels, 10–11
conflicts, delay in resolving, 35
Congreve, William, 166
connections, flight, 235, 236
consents, 5
Consumer Reports, 28, 116, 185,
194, 201, 221–2
contacts list, 79, 86, 87–8, 92, 200,
208, 239
contractors, 32
contracts, 42, 194, 202
conversations, avoiding, 62
cooking, 35, 113–14, 115, 117, 150,
180, 189
cooling, 195
cooperatives, 99
cop-outs, 21
cords
extension, 196, 227
laptop, 227
telephone, 81
corkscrew, 186
correspondence
dictating, 217
filing, 14, 202
on laptops, 92, 239
personal, 203, 207
software, 89
in spare time, 18, 38
travel, 76, 230
cost, opportunity, 51
coupons, 211
couriers, 46, 82, 104, 245
credit cards, 176, 183, 230
for booking hotels, 243
corporate, 61–2

for furnishings, 185
for gifts, 148–9
Internet, 21, 49, 85, 90, 96–8,
135–6, 139, 175, 183, 185
from limited number of vendors,
9
logging, 11
lottery tickets purchased near,
141
near parking availability, 220
as time thief, 35
websites, 104
see also specific shopping
websites in text
Shortcut Chicken, *126*
shortcuts
desktop, 107, 109, 111
for using devices, 13
shorthand, 68
Short-lived Stir-fry Beef, *126*
Short-order Scallops, *126–7*
showers, 17, 168
Shrimp en Buisson, *133*
Shrimp Scamper, *127*
signs, 20
simplifying, 8
sizes, clothing, 175
skiing, 24, 162
Skinner, B. F., 43–4
sleep, 40, 158–9, 163, 173, 182,
238, 239–40
Slick, Grace, 165
slide shows, 89
Smead Inc., 210
smoke detectors, 201
smoking, 144, 163
snacks, 114, 150, 151, 219, 238,
243
socializing, 29, 41
Social Security Administration, 101
socks, 184, 192, 228
sofabeds, 185

software, computer, 106–12
anti-virus, 112
automatic dating in, 62
backup of, 5
banking, 59
bill-paying, 199
buying, 51
communications, 90
computers and, 93
for contacts list, 88
date/time and, 32
faxing, 71
fitness, 161
for home office, 207–8
ID numbers for, 6
for labels, 74, 204
for managing contacts, 86
OCR (Optical Character
Recognition), 90
Personal Information Manager
(PIM), 31
preloaded, 91
project folders in, 64
reference, 63
registering, 100
shared files in, 61
synchronization of, 92
tax, 210
for telecommuting, 65
time for learning, 91, 111
for To-Do lists, 30
user manuals for, 13
voice-mail, 87
websites, 98
solicitors, 34, 82, 86, 152
solitude, 154
Sony Corporation, 217
sorting
laundry, 192
mail, 18, 22
papers, 68
speakerphone, 14, 17, 49, 85, 110,